Frederick Oakeley

Catholic Worship

a manual of popular instruction on the ceremonies and devotions of the church

Frederick Oakeley

Catholic Worship
a manual of popular instruction on the ceremonies and devotions of the church

ISBN/EAN: 9783337286408

Printed in Europe, USA, Canada, Australia, Japan

Cover: Foto ©Lupo / pixelio.de

More available books at **www.hansebooks.com**

CATHOLIC WORSHIP:

A

Manual of Popular Instruction

ON THE

CEREMONIES AND DEVOTIONS OF THE CHURCH.

BY

FREDERICK CANON OAKELEY, M.A.

MISSIONARY RECTOR OF ST. JOHN'S, ISLINGTON.

'And I John saw the holy city Jerusalem coming down out of heaven from God, prepared as a bride adorned for her husband.'

Apoc. xxi. 2.

With Permission.

SECOND EDITION.

NEW YORK:

THE CATHOLIC PUBLICATION SOCIETY,

9 WARREN STREET.

1872.

ADVERTISEMENT TO THE FIRST EDITION

The following little book is intended as a sequel to one published by its compiler many years ago in a catechetical form, entitled 'The Order and Ceremonial of the Most Holy Sacrifice of the Mass explained in a Dialogue between a Priest and a Catechumen.' It will be found to contain a good deal of information already supplied by its predecessor; but the compiler has thought it better to risk the charge of superfluous repetition than to make constant references to a book which his readers might not have before them.

It is hardly necessary to add that the present work, like that of which it forms the sequel, is intended, not for the direction of Priests or the information of experienced Catholics, but for the assistance of recent converts and non-Catholic inquirers. Though it presents what its compiler believes to be the most approved construction of the rubrics, his object has been that rather of exhibiting the general practice of the Church (except where otherwise noted) than of adjusting such practice with the proper standards. The care now bestowed in this country on the orderly conduct of Divine Worship goes far to supersede the necessity of any such adjustment.

Two or three quotations have been made in the following pages from a volume of sacred poetry, lately published under the title of *Lyra Liturgica.* The object of that work was in many ways illustrative of the one now presented to the public; while not a little will be found in this manual which is illustrative of its poetical companion. By a comparison between these two works of one common author, the reader will at all events understand the light in which that author humbly conceives that the ceremonial provisions of the Church should be regarded; and though he does not pretend that this light is the only true one, yet, in justice to himself, and in the way of apology for so very matter-of-fact a treatise as the present, he thinks it but fair to ask that the technical and the meditative aspects of Ceremonial which he has thus tried to set forth should be used to explain one another.

The compiler cannot bring these few prefatory remarks to an end without expressing his gratitude to those numerous subscribers who have so generously encouraged his undertaking. He asked for a guarantee of 600 copies, and thought that he was asking more than he had a right to expect. But the response to his appeal has come in the form of a pledge from 136 subscribers to the extent of no fewer than 1706 copies. All he can say, in answer to this proof of confidence, is, that he has done his best to justify it.

ST. JOHN'S, ISLINGTON.
Whitsuntide 1867.

ADVERTISEMENT TO THE SECOND EDITION.

In publishing a second edition of this little manual, the compiler takes the opportunity of thanking the Catholic public for the indulgence with which it has been received. The least return which he can make for that indulgence is to take care that it shall be made as accurate as possible, and he has accordingly given it an attentive revision, with the aid of an able and experienced ceremonialist.

St. John's, Islington,
Feast of St. Ignatius, 1872.

CONTENTS.

PART IV.

Devotional Practices of the Church.

APPENDIX.

Occasional Offices of the Church.

CATHOLIC WORSHIP.

PART I.

Permanent Arrangements of the Church.

I.

INTERIOR OF A CATHOLIC CHURCH.

AT the entrance of every Catholic church, chapel, and oratory, there is placed, either in the wall or against it, a vessel of *Holy Water*,* from which Catholics entering the church are accustomed to take a few drops, with which they touch themselves on the forehead, breast, and shoulders, saying at the same time the words, 'In the name of the Father, and of the Son, and of the Holy Ghost, Amen.' The intention of this practice is twofold; first it reminds us, on entering God's House, of the Most Holy Trinity, as we repeat the invocation of the Three Persons in one God; and secondly, of the Passion and Death of God the Son, as we make on our bodies the sign of the Cross on which He died for us. It may also be regarded as symbolical, and suggestive

* See Glossary at the end. The terms explained in the Glossary are printed in *italics* the *first* time they occur in the text.

B

of the purity with which we ought to enter into the presence of God.

Every Catholic church contains at least one Altar at the principal end, which is called the High Altar, and is dedicated to God under the invocation or patronage of the Saint, Angel, or Mystery from whom or from which the church derives its name. Larger churches also contain other Altars, either placed in side chapels, or, at any rate, railed off from the body of the church. Such Altars are sometimes found in a line with the High Altar, but, according to the practice generally prevailing at Rome, they are arranged along the sides of the church, at right angles to the High Altar. The High Altar is generally elevated by three steps from the enclosed space around it, which is called the *Sanctuary*, and which is also raised above the level of the rest of the church. The side Altars are likewise raised from the floor by at least one step. These Altars, and the chapels in which they may be contained, are dedicated to God under the invocation of some divine Mystery, or some Saint to whom there are reasons for special reverence, whether on account of the universal honour of the Church, or of national or local veneration. In churches attached to Religious Communities, Saints who have belonged to the particular Order or Congregation which those communities represent have usually an Altar of their own. In churches where there is more than one Altar, there is generally an Altar dedicated to the honour of the Blessed Virgin Mary, unless the church itself should be under her invocation, in which case the High Altar will, of course, be the Altar of our Lady.

II.

THE MOST HOLY SACRAMENT.

The Blessed Sacrament is reserved in all churches for the communion of the sick and the adoration of the

Faithful. The Altar where It is kept may be known from its having one or more lamps burning before it. In parochial churches It is usually kept at the High Altar; but in cathedrals, and some other large churches, there is generally a special chapel and Altar of the Blessed Sacrament at which It is habitually kept, and from which It is removed to other Altars on certain occasions. As lamps are sometimes lighted for devotion before other Altars besides that at which the Blessed Sacrament is reserved, it may be well to mention, for the purpose of avoiding mistake, that the only certain indication of the Adorable Presence is that of a veil of silk, or other rich material, covering the *Tabernacle.* The Faithful are in the habit of making a genuflexion, that is, of going down on the right knee, whenever they pass before the Tabernacle in which the Blessed Sacrament is kept; or (should It be visible, as at Benediction or solemn Exposition) of kneeling before It on both knees. If the act of consecration in the Mass be going on, they continue to kneel during the time which is occupied by that act. It is likewise customary even for Priests, on the three latter days of Holy Week, when the crucifix alone is present on the Altar, to pay it the same outward honour as the Blessed Sacrament would otherwise receive, out of respect to the Mystery of the Passion which is then uppermost in the mind of the Church, and at all times those engaged in the public offices of the Church, except the *Celebrant* and Canons, are required to genuflect on passing before the High Altar surmounted by its crucifix. It may here be stated, once for all, that such outward bodily acts express different degrees of honour according to the object to which they are directed, and the intention of those who perform them. By kneeling before the Blessed Sacrament, or before a crucifix, Catholics mean to express an interior act of supreme adoration towards the Second Person of the Blessed Trinity, in the former case actually present under the Sacramental veils, and in the latter symbolically represented. By this act of external honour when performed towards an image of the Blessed Virgin, they mean to denote a worship or veneration infinitely lower than that which is due to God, yet far higher than they would be justified in paying towards even the most exalted of the Saints. By the same bodily act as performed towards a *relic*, or image of a Saint, they express no more than the homage due to some portion of a body which has been inhabited in a special manner by the Holy Spirit of God, or to something which has come directly into contact with such a body, or, lastly, to some visible representation and memorial of one thus signally favoured above the other servants of God.

III.

THE FURNITURE OF THE ALTARS AND SANCTUARY.

Every Altar is surmounted by a Crucifix, which is removed only when the Blessed Sacrament is exposed. The High Altar, and that of the Blessed Sacrament, always contain a receptacle for the Blessed Sacrament, which is called a Tabernacle, over which is usually a veil of silk or other rich material, which is drawn back when the Blessed Sacrament is not present, and drawn over the door of the Tabernacle when It is present; the interior of the Tabernacle is also veiled by a curtain of rich silk. The vessel in which the Blessed Sacrament is reserved for the communion of the Faithful is called a *Ciborium*, and ought to be of precious metal, or at least silvered or gilt, and to have a covering of rich white silk, or cloth of gold, when the Blessed Sacrament is contained in it. The frame in which the Blessed Sacrament is exposed is called a *Monstrance* (sometimes, less properly, Remonstrance), or *Ostensorium;* and the smaller frame in which the Blessed Sacrament Itself is placed for Exposition is called the *Lunette*.

The Monstrance should be of the same precious material as the Chalice or Ciborium, and in many churches is studded with jewels. When the Blessed Sacrament is exposed in the Monstrance, whether for a shorter or a longer time, It is raised on an elevation called a *Throne*.

Six tall candlesticks, containing wax candles, always stand on the High Altar, and at least two on other Altars. These candles are lighted at all Offices, but not at Low Mass, unless celebrated by a Prelate. When the Bishop of the diocese performs solemn Mass, a seventh is added. Other candles, to the number at least of twelve, are lighted when the Blessed Sacrament is exposed. Flowers may be placed on the Altars, except at penitential seasons, or during Masses of *Requiem.* The Altars always contain relics within them, and are covered with three white linen cloths, and during Mass three cards are placed upon them containing those parts of the Mass which it is necessary for the Priest to have immediately before him. For the rest he makes use of the Missal. The consecration always takes place on stone. The Altar is often fronted by an *Antependium* of the colour proper to the day. The variation of colours according to the day shall afterwards be explained.

The Sanctuary contains, besides the Altar, at least one small table called a *Credence*, intended for the sacred vessels and other articles required at Solemn Mass. It also contains seats for the Priests and Sacred Ministers called *Sedilia ;* and when prepared for the solemn Offices, other seats for the various attendants. In the wall of the Sanctuary, there is usually an aperture with a drain for carrying the remains of the blessed water into the ground. This is properly called a *Piscina*, and may be seen in many of our ancient, though now desecrated, churches. The Holy Oils of the year are most properly kept within the wall of the Sanctuary.

IV.

OBJECTS IN THE INTERIOR OF A CATHOLIC CHURCH INTENDED FOR RELIGIOUS USE.

Near the entrance of the church is placed the Baptismal Font, which is filled with water solemnly blessed on Holy Saturday according to a rite hereafter to be explained. The Font should be railed off, and is sometimes surmounted by a stone or wooden canopy.

The Confessionals usually consist of three compartments; that in the centre being intended for the Priest, and those at the sides for the penitents who alternately present themselves to be heard by him. Between the central and each of the lateral compartments there is a grating of close network through which the voice is audible, but which prevents any other than oral communication between the Confessor and the penitent.

Catholic churches usually contain a pulpit, though the instruction is sometimes given from the Altar. The pulpit will more generally be found on the left side in going up a church, that is to say, on the Gospel side of the Altar.

V.

OTHER OBJECTS OF DEVOTION IN A CATHOLIC CHURCH.

Catholic churches usually contain images and sacred pictures. These are often placed over the several Altars, but may also be found in other parts of the church. Among the most frequent objects of devotion belonging to this class are the series of pictures, or mural sculptures, representing different incidents in the history of our Lord's Passion, and called the *Stations of the Cross*. These are fourteen in number, beginning with our Lord's Condemnation, and ending with His Burial. When Relics are exposed on the Altars, their presence is denoted by lights burning before them.

Candles or lamps are also frequently lighted before images, at the cost of devout persons wishing to show this mark of reverence to the Saint whose image they so honour.

PART II.

Ordinary Offices of the Church.

I.

ARRANGEMENT OF THE SANCTUARY FOR HIGH MASS.

THE Antependium, as well as the curtain on the Tabernacle, should be of the same colour as the vestments, though gold is often used as a substitute for all colours excepting purple or black. Other drapery used in the church may be of any ecclesiastical colour. The large candles which always stand on the High Altar are lighted shortly before the High Mass; other candles may also be lighted on great Festivals, on a lower level. Other candles may also be lighted before the Consecration; and it is rubrical, though not customary, to light an extra candle before the consecration even at Low Masses. The Missal is placed on the Altar at the Epistle corner, open at the Mass of the day. On the credence-table are placed the *Chalice* and *Paten* duly prepared, and covered with two *veils*, the smaller one (which is called the chalice veil) with which the chalice and paten are always covered except during the more solemn portion of the Mass, and a larger one, called a *humeral veil*, used at High Mass only, to cover the shoulders of the Subdeacon while he holds the paten, between the Offertory and the Paternoster. The *burse* is placed over the veils for the convenience of removal at the proper time in the Mass. On the credence-table are also placed the *Cruets* containing the wine and water, the book from which the Epistle and Gospel are sung, and all else which is required for the Mass.

II.

PREPARATIONS FOR HIGH MASS.

The vestments used at Mass vary in colour according to the subject of the day, and in richness according to its rank in the calendar of the Church. As a general rule, the vestments used at High Mass are more costly than those used at Low Mass. The colours are five; white, red, green, purple, and black. Gold may be used instead of any of the three former colours. White, which is typical of purity, is used on all Festivals of our Lord, excepting those which relate to His Passion; and on all Festivals of our Lady without any exception. It is also used on all days sacred to the Angels, or to Saints who are not Martyrs; on the Feast of the Holy Trinity, of the Dedication of Churches, on the Sundays during the Christmas, Epiphany, and Easter seasons (except Sundays which fall within the Octave of a Martyr's day), and on week-days (kept as such) during the same seasons; also on all days of Octaves when the Festival itself requires white. Red is used on Whit Sunday and during Whitsun week, probably as symbolical of the fire in the form of which the Holy Ghost descended upon the Apostles; also, as being a symbol of blood and martyrdom, on Festivals of the Passion of our Lord, on all Martyrs' days, and on the days within their Octaves, even on Sundays. Green is used, as being the least expressive of colours, on all ordinary Sundays (not in special seasons), and on week-days not marked by any Festival or Octave, excepting in the same special seasons. Purple, which is a penitential colour, is proper to the Sundays in Advent and Lent, as well as to the week-days during those seasons, should no Festival occur on them. It is also used on the Feast of the Holy Innocents (except when it falls on a Sunday), since the Church regards this as a day of mourning, although, on the Octave day of that Feast, red is used as on ordinary Martyrs' days. Black is confined to Good Friday and All Souls' day, but is used at all Masses of the Dead.

III.

THE PROCESSION TO HIGH MASS.

In long processions, when the parochial cross is borne, the *Thurifer* precedes with the *thurible*. He is followed by the cross, borne between two *Acolyths* with lighted candles. When *Confraternities* walk in a procession, they precede the cross, that of the Blessed Sacrament, as the first in rank, coming next to it. The cross is followed by clerics, or other attendants, habited in surplice or *cotta*, those of the highest rank coming last. The procession terminates with the Celebrant, preceded by the *Deacon* and *Subdeacon*, in single file, if the Priest be habited for the Mass; if habited in cope, the Deacon and Subdeacon are at his right and left. If the Bishop of the diocese assist, he walks last, preceded by his assistant ministers; and if an Archbishop, by the Archiepiscopal cross. As the procession approaches the High Altar, the Confraternities which may be present file off, the clerics or assistants not directly engaged in the ceremony take their places in the choir after genuflecting and bowing to each other, and the Priest with his Ministers, and the Bishop if present, enter the Sanctuary, and proceed to the foot of the Altar.

IV.

THE ASPERGES.

The ceremonies of High Mass are preceded, on all Sundays throughout the year, by the *Asperges*, or sprinkling of the people with holy water previously blessed for that purpose. This ceremony is sometimes performed as a separate rite; and, in that case, the Priest enters the church attended by an assistant, and at the conclusion of the rite returns to the sacristy to vest for the High Mass. But it is more correct that the Priest with the Sacred Ministers should enter the church in procession (the Priest being vested in *cope*) and give the Asperges without returning to the sacristy before the Mass. In this case he will change his cope for the *chasuble*, in the sanctuary, when the Asperges is concluded. The rite of the Asperges is as follows. The Priest, kneeling between the Sacred Ministers on the lowest step of the Altar, receives the *aspersory* from the Deacon, sprinkles the Altar three times, touches himself with the holy water, and sprinkles the Deacon and Subdeacon on each side of him. Meanwhile he intones the words, 'Asperges me,' which the choir follows up with the remainder of the verse of the 50th Psalm, of which they form the beginning, and of which the following is a translation: 'Thou shalt sprinkle me with hyssop, and I shall be cleansed; Thou shalt wash me, and I shall be whiter than snow.' The choir then sings the Gloria Patri (except in Passion-tide), and repeats at least the first portion of the verse. Should there be a Bishop in the sanctuary, the Priest gives him the aspersory to touch; he then goes from the sanctuary into the church, attended by his Ministers, and sprinkles the people on either side, after which he returns into the sanctuary, and sings the prescribed *versicles* and prayer, of which the following are translations:

'*V.* O Lord, show us Thy mercy.
R. And grant us Thy salvation.
V. O Lord, hear my prayer.
R. And let my cry come unto Thee.
V. The Lord be with you.
R. And with thy spirit.

Let us pray.

Hear us, Holy Lord, Almighty Father, Everlasting God, and vouchsafe to send Thy holy Angel from heaven to guard, cherish, protect, and defend all who inhabit this dwelling-place, through Christ our Lord. Amen.'

During the Easter Season—that is, from Easter-day to Whitsunday both inclusive—the following Antiphon is substituted for that used at other times: 'I saw water going forth from the Temple on the right side, and all to whom that water came received salvation. Alleluia, Alleluia.'

Alleluia is also added to the versicle, 'O Lord, show us,' &c., with its response.

The object of this ceremony is to impress on the people an idea of the purity with which they ought to assist at High Mass, the most solemn Office of the Church.

V.

THE HIGH MASS.

It should be observed, for the instruction of strangers, that High Mass is merely the more solemn celebration of the great Eucharistic Sacrifice, which, when offered without those more solemn accompaniments, is called Low Mass. For a description of what is common to both celebrations, I must refer the reader to a little book which I published several years ago under the title of 'The Order and Ceremonial of the Most Holy and Adorable Sacrifice of the Mass.' I will here specify those ceremonies only which are peculiar to High Mass.

The Priest who celebrates, having exchanged the cope for the chasuble at the Sedilia, where the Deacon and Subdeacon have also assumed their *maniples* (or, if there be no Asperges, having proceeded in his chasuble from the sacristy), goes with his Ministers to the foot of the Altar, where he begins the Mass, the Deacon and Subdeacon making together the responses, which at a Low Mass are made by the *Server*. All three then ascend to the *predella* of the Altar, while the thurifer comes up on the Epistle side with the thurible, into which the Celebrant puts incense three times, and afterwards blesses it in these words: 'Mayest thou be blessed by Him in whose honour thou shalt be burned.' He then receives the thurible from the Deacon, and incenses the cross over the Altar, and afterwards the Altar itself, both above and below on each side. He is then himself incensed by the Deacon, and afterwards proceeds to read the *Introit* of the Mass, and say the *Kyrie* with the Sacred Ministers. All three either remain at the corner of the Altar, or go to the Sedilia, according to the custom of different churches.

When the Priest and his Ministers begin the Mass, the choir sings the words of the Introit, and afterwards the Kyrie. When the choir has concluded the Kyrie, the Celebrant goes to the middle of the Altar and intones the *Gloria in excelsis*. The Deacon and Subdeacon, who have previously stood behind him, one behind the other, then go up to his right and left at the Altar and recite the *Gloria* with him, after which act the three retire to the Sedilia, and remain seated till the choir has ended the 'Gloria.' At the words 'Adoramus Te,' 'Gratias agimus Tibi,' 'Jesu Christi,' and 'Suscipe deprecationem nostram,' which are especially expressive of reverence, they take off their *birettas*, and incline the head at a signal from the *Master of Ceremonies*. The choir having ended the 'Gloria,' the Celebrant and Sacred Ministers return to the Altar, where the Celebrant sings the collect or collects of the day, and afterwards reads the Epistle and Gospel, which are respectively sung by the Subdeacon and Deacon, the former of whom receives the benediction of the Celebrant after singing the Epistle, and the later before singing the Gospel.

Between the Epistle and Gospel the Celebrant will have recited the *Gradual* or *Tract*, and, on certain days, the proper *Sequence*, all of which should be sung by the choir. Previously to the singing of the Gospel, the Celebrant puts incense into the thurible for the use of the Deacon, who incenses the book from which he sings the Gospel, while the choir is responding 'Glory be to Thee, O Lord,' in answer to the announcement of the Gospel of the day. When the Deacon has ended the Gospel, the Subdeacon carries the book from which he has sung it to the Celebrant, who kisses the beginning of the text, saying at the same time, 'By the evangelical words may our offences be blotted out.' The Celebrant is then incensed by the Deacon, and, if there be a sermon or instruction, the Deacon and Subdeacon accompany the Celebrant to the Sedilia, where they remain seated till the instruction is ended. If there be no instruction, the Celebrant, as soon as he has been incensed after the Gospel, goes to the middle of the Altar and intones the *Credo*, and is joined, as at the 'Gloria,' by the Sacred Ministers, who proceed to recite it with him, and then go down with him to the Sedilia, where all three remain seated till the choir (which begins the music of the 'Credo' as soon as the Celebrant has intoned the first words) has finished it. At the words 'Jesum Christum' (if sung after the Celebrant and his Ministers are seated) they bare their heads. At the 'Et incarnatus est' they also remain uncovered and inclined, till after the words, 'Et Homo factus est.' On Christmas Day, and on the Feast of the Annunciation, they kneel during the same words, out of reverence to the great Mystery of the Incarnation, then specially commemorated. The Celebrant and his Ministers also bare their heads at the word 'Adoratur.' When the 'Et incarnatus est,' and words immediately following, have been sung, the Deacon receives the burse, carries it to the Altar, and spreads the *Corporal*. Just before the choir has concluded, the three return to the Altar. When the Celebrant has sung 'Dominus vobiscum' and 'Oremus,' the Deacon goes to his right, and the Subdeacon to the credence-table, where he takes the chalice and paten, and brings them under the humeral veil (with which he has been invested by the Master of Ceremonies) to the Altar, where the Deacon uncovers them, gives the paten to the Celebrant to offer the bread, pours wine into the chalice, to which the Subdeacon adds a small quantity of water (previously blessed by the Celebrant), and then assists the Celebrant in offering the chalice. This mingling of wine and water in the chalice is supposed to be commemorative of the Blood and Water which flowed from the Sacred Side of our Lord when pierced with the lance. The Subdeacon next receives from the Deacon the paten, which he carries under the humeral veil to the foot of the Altar, where he continues to hold it, raised to the height of his eyes, till the Paternoster. The Deacon then assists the Celebrant to put incense into the thurible. The Celebrant, assisted by the Deacon, incenses the bread and wine, and afterwards the Crucifix and Altar, as at the beginning of the Mass, excepting that he now uses certain special words, both in blessing the incense, and incensing the Altar. While blessing the incense he says, 'May the Lord, through the intercession of St. Michael the Archangel standing at the right hand of the Altar of incense, and of all His elect, vouchsafe to bless this incense, and to receive it as an odour of sweetness, through Christ our Lord. Amen.' At the incensation of the bread and wine he says, 'May this incense, which Thou hast blessed, ascend to Thee, O Lord, and may Thy mercy descend upon us.' At that of the Crucifix and Altar he says, 'Let my prayer, O Lord, be directed as incense in Thy sight, and the lifting up of my hands as an evening sacrifice. Set a watch, O Lord, before my mouth, and a door round about my lips. Incline not my heart to evil words, to make excuses in sin.' He then gives the thurible to the Deacon, saying the words, 'May the Lord enkindle within us the fire of His love, and the flame of everlasting Charity. Amen.' The Deacon then incenses the Celebrant, and afterwards the choir and Subdeacon, and is himself incensed by the thurifer. At the conclusion of the *Preface*, the Deacon and Subdeacon go up to the right and left of the Celebrant, and say with him the *Sanctus*. Immediately after the Sanctus has been said by the Priest, lights are brought into the Sanctuary for the *Elevation*, and taken away when it is over, except in Masses of the Dead, and when Communion is given, at which they remain till after the Communion. At the Elevation all kneel, but the Deacon rises to remove the *pall* from the chalice, and to replace it. Towards the end of the Paternoster the Subdeacon goes up to the Altar, resigns the paten, and is divested of the humeral veil. At the 'Pax Domini' he again goes up to the Altar to recite the *Agnus Dei* with the Celebrant and Deacon. When the Celebrant has concluded the first of the three prayers before communion, he gives to the Deacon the '*pax*,' or kiss of peace, which the Deacon afterwards gives to the Subdeacon, and he to the Senior Cleric on each side of the choir, by whom it is given to the rest, and so on throughout the whole choir. It is in the same way circulated among the assistants in the Sanctuary. After the *Ablutions* the chalice and paten are re-arranged by the Subdeacon, who carries them to the credence-table. The Mass then proceeds to its conclusion. The 'Ite missa est' is sung by the Deacon to a tone prescribed in the Missal, and varying on different days; he and the Subdeacon then kneel to receive the blessing, unless they be both Canons, in which case they bow their heads. When the last Gospel has been said by the Celebrant, all retire in procession in the order in which they entered.*

* In the lesser churches, where there is a paucity of Clergy,

VI.

PONTIFICAL HIGH MASS.

When High Mass is celebrated by the Bishop of the Diocese, a throne is erected for him on the Gospel side of the Altar. The *Canon* of the Mass is placed on the Altar instead of the usual cards. The Missal is borne in the procession into the church by the Subdeacon of the Mass, together with the maniple of the Bishop, which the Subdeacon presents to him to put on at the prayer 'Indulgentiam' at the beginning of the Mass. The Bishop, before ascending to the Altar, has his Assistant Priest at his right, and the Deacon and Subdeacon at his left. When the Bishop has come to the Altar and kissed it, as usual, he kisses also the first words of the Gospel of the day, presented to him by the Subdeacon. After incensing the Altar, and being himself incensed, he goes to his throne, or, if not celebrating in his own Diocese, to a *faldstool* raised from the floor on the Epistle side of the Sanctuary. He remains there till the Offertory, reading those parts of the Mass which are sung by the Deacon, Subdeacon, or choir, and intoning as usual the 'Gloria,' 'Credo,' and 'Pax vobis,' which he sings before the Collect or Collects instead of 'Dominus vobiscum,' as well as the 'Dominus vobiscum' and 'Oremus' before the Offertory. Whenever he reads, the Assistant Priest holds the *bugia* near the book, while the Deacon takes off or puts on the mitre at the proper times; before returning to the Altar he washes his hands, the Deacon and Subdeacon assisting him. The Mass proceeds as usual to the first of the three prayers before Communion; after which the Bishop gives the

---

Mass is often sung without the Sacred Ministers. In this case, the Celebrant himself sings the Gospel, and if no cleric be present, the Epistle also. Incense is not used, as a rule. A Mass thus celebrated is called a 'Missa Cantata.'

kiss of peace, not as usual to the Deacon, but to the Assistant Priest, who gives it to any Priest who may be present in the choir, as well as to the Deacon, who afterwards gives it, as usual, to the Subdeacon. The Bishop washes his hands after he has received the second of the ablutions. The Mass then concludes as usual, the Bishop giving the Pontifical instead of the ordinary blessing.

When a Bishop celebrates who is not the Bishop of the Diocese, he occupies, instead of a throne, a faldstool on a raised platform below the Altar on the Epistle side, except when he incenses the Altar at the beginning of the Mass, and except also during the whole time between the Offertory and Communion. His Assistant Priest, Deacon, and Subdeacon occupy the ordinary Sedilia.

VII.

HIGH MASS IN THE PRESENCE OF THE DIOCESAN BISHOP.

If the Bishop who assists at High Mass be the Bishop of the diocese, a raised throne is erected for him under a canopy on the Gospel side of the Sanctuary, with seats for his Assistant Priest and Deacons, and others for his various attendants. In the procession he occupies the last place, as that of the greatest dignity. He may assist either in *cappa magna* without mitre, or in cope with mitre. He blesses from the throne the water used in the Sacrifice, and the incense, as well as the Sacred Ministers of the Mass. He reads, from a Missal of his own, those portions of the Mass which are proper to the day. Before going up to his throne, he begins the Mass at the foot of the Altar, while the Celebrant and his Ministers respond. If he assist in cappa magna, he is incensed at the Offertory only; if in cope, at the beginning of the Mass and after the Gospel also. After the Gospel (or, if there be a sermon, after the sermon) his Assistant Priest, or the preacher, proclaims the Indulgence* granted by the Church to those who are present at a High Mass at which the Bishop of the diocese assists. Previously to the proclamation of the Indulgence, the Deacon of the Mass sings the *Confiteor*, and the Bishop, after having pronounced the absolution, gives the solemn blessing. As soon as the 'Sanctus' has been said by the Celebrant, the Bishop descends with his attendants from the throne, and kneels at a faldstool at the foot of the Altar till the consecration is ended. The Bishop receives the 'pax' from his Assistant Priest, who goes to the Altar to receive it from the Celebrant, and then gives it to the Bishop, who passes it to his Assistant Deacons.

VIII.

HIGH MASS, WITH EXPOSITION OF THE BLESSED SACRAMENT.

The principal differences between an ordinary High Mass and a High Mass with Exposition of the Blessed Sacrament, are the following: the Priest consecrates two *Hosts;* one for the Mass, and the other for the Monstrance, unless the Blessed Sacrament be exposed during the whole of the Mass. During the time, whatever it may be, that the Blessed Sacrament is exposed, the Celebrant and his Ministers genuflect in those parts of the Mass where otherwise they would bow, and kneel, on approaching and quitting the Altar. It will be observed also that the Blessed Sacrament is always incensed on the knees, and that the Celebrant, instead of being himself incensed, or washing his fingers in the usual place at the Epistle corner of the Altar, descends a step, and is so incensed or washes the fingers as not to turn his back upon the Blessed Sacrament. During the Exposition of the *Forty Hours* the hand-bell is not rung at any Mass celebrated in the church.

* See Part IV. 'Indulgences.'

IX.

PROCESSION OF THE BLESSED SACRAMENT.

When a procession of the Blessed Sacrament takes place after High Mass, the Celebrant, having exchanged his chasuble for a cope, incenses the Blessed Sacrament before It is removed from the Altar, and is then vested in a veil, under which he receives the Monstrance, on his knees, from the Deacon, and carries It under a *baldacchino* through the church, or, if so be, into the open air. The choir precedes, singing the 'Pange lingua' and other hymns appropriate to the Most Holy Sacrament. On the return of the procession, the Deacon places the Monstrance on the Throne, and when the doxology of the hymn begins, assists the Priest with the thurible, and the Blessed Sacrament is incensed by the Priest as at Benediction. The Priest having sung the usual prayer, and been vested with the humeral veil, goes to the predella of the Altar, where he receives the Monstrance, on his knees, from the Deacon, and gives benediction with It to the assembled people.

At the Exposition of the 'Forty Hours,' the Litanies are sung after the procession on the day of Exposition, when no benediction is given, and before it on the day of Deposition.*

X.

HIGH MASS OF REQUIEM.

High Mass of Requiem, or of the Dead, differs from the ordinary High Mass in the following particulars: the Altar is not incensed at the beginning of the Mass, but at the Offertory alone. The Celebrant and Sacred Ministers consequently proceed at once, after ascending

* At Rome, and in some churches in this country, the Blessed Sacrament is never moved from place to place except under a small canopy.

the steps of the Altar, to the Epistle corner, where the Celebrant reads the Introit, not making the sign of the cross on his own person, but towards the book. He then says the Kyrie, and sings the collect or collects. The Subdeacon does not receive his blessing after the Epistle, nor the Deacon before the Gospel. After the Celebrant has read the 'Dies iræ,' he and the Sacred Ministers go to the Sedilia, and remain seated while it is sung by the choir. Towards the close, they rise and proceed to the Altar, where the Celebrant reads the Gospel, and the Deacon prepares to sing it. The candles are not carried to the place at which the Gospel is sung, nor is incense used. The water is not blessed before it is infused into the chalice, nor does the Subdeacon carry the paten to its place at the foot of the Altar. He therefore assists the Celebrant at the incensation of the Altar, and, together with the Deacon (who is also at liberty, because he does not, as at an ordinary High Mass, incense the choir), supplies the water and towel, instead of the acolyths, at the *Lavabo*. He also incenses the Blessed Sacrament at the Elevation, an office which, when he holds the paten, is discharged by the Master of Ceremonies. The 'pax' is not given, nor the blessing at the end of the Mass. At Masses of the Dead, and some others previously specified, the lights brought in at the 'Sanctus,' and usually taken away after the Consecration, remain in the Sanctuary till after the Communion.

XI.

SOLEMN VESPERS.

The procession into the church at Solemn *Vespers* is the same as at High Mass, excepting that the officiating Priest always wears a cope. On the greater Festivals, and in larger churches, he is often attended by assistants also wearing copes; but usually his attendants wear surplices or cottas only. There should be two *Chanters*, who are also allowed to wear copes, of a material inferior to those of the clergy. On entering the choir, the clergy and others arrange themselves on either side, while the chanters occupy high stools facing the Altar. The officiating Priest, after saying the preparatory prayers on his knees at the foot of the Altar, goes to the Sedilia, where he recites in silence the 'Pater' and 'Ave,' and intones the opening words, 'Deus in adjutorium,' &c. The principal chanter then comes up to him and sings the first words of the first Antiphon, which the Priest repeats, and the choir follows up.* The first words of the remaining Antiphons are given out in succession by the clergy present. At the conclusion of each Antiphon, the chanter intones the first words of the following psalm, and the choir on either side proceed to chant the alternate verses of each of the five psalms. The psalms being ended, the Priest sings the *capitulum*, and the principal chanter then comes up to him to announce the first words of the Hymn,† which he repeats, and the hymn is then continued by the choir in alternate stanzas. The chanter then sings the Versicle, to which the choir responds; after which the chanter goes up to the Priest, and gives him the first words of the Antiphon before the 'Magnificat,' as he had previously done with the first Antiphon. When the choir begins the 'Magnificat,' the Priest makes the sign of the cross, and goes to the Altar, which he incenses, saying the 'Magnificat.' Other Altars of the church also are sometimes incensed. When the incensation of the Altar or Altars is completed, the Priest returns to the

* *i. e.* when the Vespers are of a *Double* Festival; when of a *Semidouble*, the entire Antiphon is not sung till the end of its Psalm, or of the 'Magnificat.' In the *commemorations*, the whole Antiphon is always sung.

† At the first stanza of the hymns 'Veni Creator' and 'Ave maris Stella,' which are direct addresses to God or the Blessed Virgin, all kneel; also at the Invocation of the Cross in the hymn 'Vexilla Regis.'

Sedilia, and is himself incensed by the principal Assistant, who afterwards proceeds, with the thurifer, to incense the clergy and choir, and, lastly, the second Assistant. He then gives up the thurible to the thurifer, by whom he is himself incensed, and afterwards the other assistants and the people. The 'Magnificat' being ended, and its Antiphon repeated, the Priest sings the collect of the day; and, if other Festivals be commemorated, the collects of those Festivals also, preceded by the proper Antiphon, Versicle, and Response. After the 'Dominus vobiscum' has been repeated, the chanter sings 'Benedicamus Domino' (to which, during Easter Week, two alleluias are added), and is answered by the choir (under the same condition), 'Deo gratias;' after which the Priest sings the short prayer for the repose of the faithful departed. It is usual in this country, when the Vespers are not immediately followed by Complin, to sing the short hymn to the Blessed Virgin proper to the season; but, if Complin succeed, this hymn is sung at the close of that office.

In some churches the Vespers are chanted in the organ-gallery, in which case the Antiphons are given out without the ceremonies here described. In Rome, and in some churches elsewhere, the psalms are sung on certain great Festivals to pieces of concerted music. The ceremonies of Solemn Lauds are precisely the same as those of Solemn Vespers.

XII.

COMPLIN.

Complin is the last Office of the day, and, unlike the rest, does not vary, except very slightly, according to the season. It is most properly sung by the Priest in his place in the choir, and without solemn accompaniments, the officiating Priest being habited simply as a cleric. It begins with an invitation for a blessing, made by the chanter to the Priest, to which the Priest responds in the words, 'May God Almighty grant us a quiet night, and a perfect end.' The chanter then sings a short address, and the Priest, after singing, *V.* 'Our help is in the Name of the Lord,' *R.* 'Who made heaven and earth,' proceeds to say the Confession and prayers of Absolution; after which the Priest sings 'Deus in adjutorium.' The Psalms are then chanted alternately by the choir, with the Antiphon repeated in full; then follow the Capitulum, Hymn, Responsaries, and the 'Nunc dimittis' with its Antiphon; after which the Priest sings the Collect and Blessing; which is followed by the Hymn of the Blessed Virgin already mentioned. On *semidoubles* and week-days the Paternoster, Credo, and certain *versicles* and responses are introduced between the 'Nunc dimittis' and the Collect.

XIII.

BENEDICTION OF THE MOST HOLY SACRAMENT.

The Benediction of the Most Holy Sacrament is the most frequent rite of the Church, with the exception of the Holy Mass. It usually follows Vespers or Complin, as well as other public devotions, and is often celebrated alone. The Priest, vested in white or gold* cope and stole, and attended by two Assistants, kneels at the foot of the Altar, while the senior Assistant (usually a Priest wearing a stole†) goes up to the Altar, spreads the corporal, takes the Blessed Sacrament out of the Tabernacle, places It on the corporal, makes his adoration, then places It on the 'throne,' returns to the officiating Priest, assists him while he puts incense into the thurible, with which the Priest incenses the Blessed Sacrament three times. When the Deacon opens the door of

* When Benediction immediately follows Vespers, the cope of the Vespers may be retained, but white is always proper.

† A Deacon with stole may assist.

the Tabernacle, it is usual in this country for the choir to sing the hymn 'O Salutaris,' which is generally followed by the Litany of the Blessed Virgin, or some psalm or piece of music appropriate to the day. Afterwards is intoned the first line of the hymn 'Tantum ergo,' which the choir continues. At the beginning of the second stanza the Priest again puts incense into the thurible, and incenses the Blessed Sacrament three times, as before. When the hymn is ended, the versicle and response 'Panem de cœlo,' &c., are given out, and the Priest sings the collect. A veil is then placed on his shoulders, and the Assistant Priest or Deacon having taken down the Blessed Sacrament from the throne, the Priest receives It into his hands, and blesses the people with It in the form of a cross. A Bishop giving Benediction blesses the people in the same form three times. The Priest assisting, or Deacon, then replaces the Blessed Sacrament in the Tabernacle, folds and puts up the corporal, returns to the Priest, and all retire. Benediction may be given with the Blessed Sacrament in the Ciborium. In this case the door of the Tabernacle is opened, the inner veil withdrawn, and the Blessed Sacrament incensed. The door remains open, but the Ciborium is not taken out till the Benediction is given with it. During the Easter season and the Octave of Corpus Christi one alleluia is added to the versicle and response, as well as to those which follow the 'Te Deum,' should it be sung.

At Pontifical Benediction, and on other solemn occasions, the Assistants wear the sacred vestments.

PART III.

Offices proper to certain Seasons.

I.

FEAST OF THE PURIFICATION OF THE BLESSED VIRGIN MARY.

Previously to the High Mass on this day, candles are solemnly blessed and distributed, first to the clergy, and then to the people, by the officiating Priest. During the distribution, the choir sings the 'Nunc dimittis,' repeating the third verse, in which that 'light' of the Gospel is mentioned of which the ceremonies of this day are symbolical. The candles are afterwards lighted and borne in procession through the church, the choir singing in the procession certain prescribed antiphons. On the return of the procession the candles are extinguished, and the High Mass is celebrated. The candles are again lighted and borne in the hand during the singing of the Gospel, and also from the Sanctus to the Communion.

II.

ASH-WEDNESDAY.

Previously to the High Mass on this day, the officiating Priest blesses the Ashes in the form prescribed, and with the prayers appointed in the Missal. The ashes are made from the Palms blessed the previous year, which are burned for that purpose. The Priest first receives the sacred ashes from the principal cleric present, and then places them on the heads of the Sacred Ministers, and on those of the other clergy, and of the people, the choir in the mean time singing penitential antiphons. As the Priest places the ashes on the head of each, he says in Latin the words, 'Remember, mortal, that thou art dust, and into dust shalt return.' High Mass is afterwards celebrated according to the *ferial rite.*

III.

PASSION-TIDE.

During Passion-tide all pictures, crosses, and images in the church are veiled in purple, both in token of grief and to signify that during this time Christ walked no more openly amongst the Jews, and that His glory was obscured and hidden under persecution. At Masses of the season, the psalm 'Judica,' with which the Mass usually begins, is omitted, as well as the 'Gloria Patri,' in all parts of the Mass. On all the Sundays in Lent (except the fourth or Midlent Sunday) the Deacon and Subdeacon wear chasubles folded up in front, instead of the proper habits of their Orders. The Subdeacon takes off the chasuble before singing the Epistle, and resumes it afterwards; the Deacon takes it off before singing the Gospel, and does not resume it till after the Communion, but wears in the mean time a broad purple stole over that with which he is already invested. The 'Gloria in excelsis' is omitted in Lent, as in Advent and on Holy Innocents' Day, and 'Benedicamus Domino' substituted at the end of the Mass for 'Ite missa est.'

IV.

PALM SUNDAY.

Previously to the High Mass on this day palm-branches are solemnly blessed, distributed, and borne in procession, in memory of our Blessed Lord's entry into Jerusalem on the Sunday before His Passion, when the children of Israel met Him with palm-branches, strewing their garments in His path. The rite of their benediction differs from those of the benediction of the candles and ashes in having certain features of the Mass itself interwoven into it. There is a special Lesson and Gospel, and a proper Preface, followed by the Sanctus.

After the palms have been blessed and distributed, they are borne in procession outside the church, the choir singing the prescribed antiphons. Before the procession returns to the church a portion of the choir is admitted within the door, and sings, alternately with those who remain outside, the hymn which will be found in the office of Holy Week. When the procession has reëntered the church, High Mass is begun. On this day, as on Good Friday (as well as on the Tuesday and Wednesday in Holy Week, if High Mass be celebrated on those days), the Passion of our Lord is sung before the Gospel of the day, according to a prescribed rite. Three Deacons (or Priests so vested, but without dalmatic or folded chasuble) enter the Sanctuary at the end of the Tract, and going to that part of it where the Gospel is usually sung, proceed to chant the narrative of the Passion from the Gospel. The part of our Lord is sustained by one of the Deacons, that of single speakers in the narrative by another, while the third chants the history of the events. At Rome, and in some churches in this country, the part of the multitude is sustained by the choir, who respond in certain beautiful and expressive pieces of harmonised music. In churches where this practice does not prevail, the Deacon who takes the part of the single speaker takes that also of the multitude. Where the proper number of Deacons, or Priests acting as Deacons, cannot be provided, the part of our Lord can be chanted by the Celebrant at the Altar, who, in any case, recites the whole of the Passion. When the Passion is concluded, the Deacon of the Mass sings the Gospel, but without the customary announcement, and without the accompaniment of lights. The Mass then proceeds to the end as usual, the palms being borne in the hand during the Passion and Gospel.

V.

THE TENEBRÆ OFFICE.

On the Wednesday, Thursday, and Friday afternoons or evenings of Holy Week is sung what is called the Office of Tenebræ, consisting of the Matins and Lauds proper to those days, accompanied with special ceremonies. The name Tenebræ ('darkness') is supposed to refer, either to the supernatural darkness at the Crucifixion, or to the extinction of the lights at the end of the Office, symbolical of it, which is hereafter to be described. The Office begins abruptly by the recitation of the first antiphon and psalm, followed by the other psalms with their respective antiphons. No musical instruments are allowed to accompany the chant. When the psalms of the first *Nocturn* are concluded, a portion of the Lamentations of Jeremiah is sung in three lessons to a beautiful and plaintive tone. The Lessons of the second Nocturn are taken from St. Austin, and those of the third from the Epistles of St. Paul. At the conclusion of each of the nine psalms of Matins, and the five of Lauds, a candle is extinguished on a triangular stand placed in the Sanctuary, at the top of which one candle remains to be extinguished later. The Lauds follow the Matins without any interruption, and begin with the antiphon of the first psalm. The psalms of Lauds are followed immediately by the 'Benedictus' with its proper antiphon. At each of the last six verses of the 'Benedictus,' one of the six large candles on the Altar is extinguished, and, ultimately, all other lights in the church, with the exception only of the topmost candle on the triangular stand. This is afterwards carried and hidden under the Epistle corner of the Altar, while the choir sings the words, 'Christ was made obedient for us unto death.' On the second day are added the words, 'Even the death of the cross;' and on the third, 'Wherefore

God hath exalted Him, and given Him a Name which is above every name.' When the words, 'Christ was made,' &c. are begun, all kneel, and continue kneeling till the end of the Office. When they are concluded, the officiating Priest says the Paternoster secretly, and then recites, with the choir, in a low tone of voice, the psalm 'Miserere.' He then repeats the collect in the same tone, but without the usual ending. A slight noise is afterwards made, in reference, probably, to the earthquake and confusion of nature which occurred at the Crucifixion, the candle is brought back from the Altar, and replaced in the triangular stand, and all retire. In Rome the psalm 'Miserere' is sung to harmonised music.

The words of the Tenebræ Office vary on each of the three days, but its structure and ceremonies are always the same.

VI.

HOLY THURSDAY.

The Thursday in Holy Week called Holy Thursday (or sometimes in England Maundy Thursday) is kept as the Feast of the Last Supper. One Mass only (which should be a High Mass) is celebrated in each church on this day, and the earlier portion of it with accompaniments of joyful solemnity, which render it an exception to the otherwise mournful ceremonies of the week. The High Altar, with its Tabernacle and Crucifix, is vested in white, and the vestments of the Mass are white or gold. Additional lights are placed on the Altar in honour of the Blessed Sacrament. In another part of the church, an Altar is richly adorned with lights and flowers in profusion. Over this Altar is placed a receptacle for the Blessed Sacrament, which is frequently in the shape of an *ark* or sarcophagus, gilt or richly carved. This is intended to receive within it the Blessed Sacrament after Its removal from the Altar where the High Mass is celebrated, and to contain It till the end of the Office on the morning of Good Friday. The chapel thus prepared is frequently called the Chapel of the Sepulchre, but more properly the *Altar of Repose*.

At the Mass, the introductory psalm 'Judica,' always used by the Priest before ascending to the Altar (except during Passion-tide and in Masses of the Dead), is omitted. As soon as the Celebrant has intoned the 'Gloria in excelsis,' the organ strikes up, and the hand-bell used in the Mass is rung continuously till he has ended the recitation of the 'Gloria.' The outer bells of the church are also sounded. When the Priest has ended the 'Gloria,' the inner bell ceases, but the bells of the church may continue sounding till the choir has finished the music. The organ then ceases, and no musical instrument is afterwards allowed in the Mass or Office till after the intonation of the 'Gloria' on Holy Saturday. Two Hosts are consecrated; one for the Mass, and the other for removal to the Altar where the Blessed Sacrament is to remain till the morrow. The 'Agnus Dei' is not said, nor is the kiss of peace given. When the Celebrant has received the Communion of the Precious Blood, he places the unconsumed Host, with the assistance of the Deacon, in a chalice other than that which has been used in the Mass, and covers it with a pall and inverted paten, over which is thrown a veil of silk or cloth-of-gold.

The Deacon, having assisted the Celebrant in arranging the Chalice for the Altar of reservation, uncovers the Ciborium, and proceeds to sing the 'Confiteor,' after which the Celebrant says the two prayers of absolution. The Deacon then returns, and with the Subdeacon receives the Holy Communion first of all. It is then administered to the Clergy present (those who are Priests wearing stoles), and afterwards to the laity.*

* It is the intention of the Church that a general Communion of the Faithful should take place during the Mass of this day, in memory of Christ having distributed His Sacred Body and Blood

At the conclusion of the Mass, the Celebrant exchanges his chasuble for a cope, and proceeds to the foot of the Altar. At the same time a baldacchino or canopy is brought to the entrance of the Sanctuary, borne by Priests, Laics of high rank, or members of the Confraternity of the Blessed Sacrament, accompanied by attendants bearing lights. The Priest, having put incense into the thuribles, incenses the Blessed Sacrament in the chalice on the Altar, and then receives It on his knees from the hands of the Deacon, the hymn 'Pange lingua' being immediately intoned. The Priest then bears the Blessed Sacrament under the canopy in

---

to His Apostles at His last supper, though, on account of the late hour at which the Mass is often celebrated in this country, the practice has grown up of giving Communion out of Mass at an earlier hour. Since, however, it is desired in this work to represent the normal as well as the actual practice of the Church, and since in Collegiate and some other churches such normal practice prevails among us, it has been considered best to describe it.

It may be well in this place to make two observations with the view of meeting objections often urged by ill-informed persons against matters of Catholic institution or practice. It is commonly said that the Church denies the Chalice to the Laity, as if she reserved it in some jealous or exclusive spirit to the Clergy. But the fact is, as may be known to any one present at the general Communion on Holy Thursday, that Priests who go to Communion, as well as all other persons, receive under one Species alone. The distinction is not between the Priests and the Laity, but between the *Celebrant* at Mass and all other persons, whether Priests or not. Again, those strangers to the Church, who attend High Mass only, often go away with the impression that Catholics do not frequently go to Communion, because they do not communicate at High Mass, except on Holy Thursday, and some other rare occasions; the fact being that, as a strict natural fast is a necessary condition of receiving the Holy Communion, the Faithful, according to a practice which admits but of few exceptions, go to Communion at early Low Masses. Thus, on Easter Sunday, for instance, several hundred persons have already received the Communion at an earlier hour, in those larger churches which are most frequently visited at the High Mass on that great festival by non-Catholics, who are seldom present in our churches at other times. The same is true of all Catholic churches, in proportion to the numbers who are attached to them.

procession to the Altar of Repose, the choir continuing the hymn, and two or more thurifers incensing the path of the Blessed Sacrament with their faces towards It. When the procession has reached the Altar of the reservation, the Deacon receives from him the Blessed Sacrament, and places It in the Ark, the Priest incensing It before the ark is closed. When the ark has been locked, the procession returns, without the canopy, to the High Altar, where the choir remain to chant the Vespers of the day, which the officiating Priest says at the same time with his Ministers in the Sacristy. Towards the close of the public Vespers, the officiating Priest, accompanied by the Deacon, both habited in purple stoles, and attended by clerks, proceeds to strip the High Altar, and other Altars of the church, while the choir chants the 21st Psalm, in which occur the words, 'They have divided My garments amongst them, and upon My vesture they have cast lots.' Should the Blessed Sacrament have remained at the High Altar after the Mass, a Priest will previously have removed It. The Holy Water is likewise removed from the church, and not restored till Holy Saturday.

The great attraction in the church during the remainder of this day will be the Sepulchre or Altar of Repose, at which the Most Holy Sacrament is reserved till the morrow, for the loving adoration of those who seek by their devotion to make reparation for the indignities of the Passion. This thought has been illustrated in some lines of poetry which the author may be pardoned for introducing in connection with these more technical details :*

The notes of joy have died away,
Sweet bell and organ shrill,
As gather round the Light of Day
The clouds of coming ill.

* *Lyra Liturgica:* Holy Thursday. (Burns.)

The Feast is o'er, and Thou art fain
  Thy Passion to begin;
And Judas covenants for gain
  To work his work of sin.

The ruffian bands his call await,
  With staff, and sword, and lance;
And now they near the garden-gate,
  And stealthily advance.

I hear the armour's sullen clash
  Break on the stilly night;
I see the torches' lurid flash
  Flouting the pale moonlight.

Sweet Saviour! 'tis the time for us
  To rally round Thy throne;
The rebel world may treat Thee thus,
  But we are still Thine own.

Then come, ye servants of the Lord,
  And reverently bring
The choicest of your sacred hoard
  To grace your glorious King.

The air that floats around His head
  With odorous clouds imbue;
The ground that feels His sov'reign tread
  With flowers of spring bestrew.

Let guards His royal path escort,
  Let warning lights be there;
But not the traitor's fell cohort—
  But not the torches' glare.

Come, O ye choirs, your voices raise
  As He is borne on high;
And drown with notes of Christian praise
  The rabble's furious cry.

So let us bring Him home, and there
Our meek devotion pay;
And travel o'er, in faith and prayer,
That bitter night and day;

Nor share the blame those slumbering three
On heedless watchers drew:
'Could ye not wake one hour with Me,
Who bear the Cross for you?'*

The Consecration of the Oils.

On Holy Thursday in each year the Bishop of the diocese consecrates the Sacramental Oils for the use of the Church. This solemn ceremony takes place during the High Mass of the day in the Cathedral Church, or elsewhere, according to the choice of the Diocesan. The Holy Oils are three in number: viz. the Chrism, the Baptismal Oil (or Oil of the *Catechumens*), and the Oil of the Sick.

The oils are prepared in the Sacristy in three large vessels of silver, or plated metal (that for the Chrism being the largest of the three), covered with veils, which, in the case of the oil for the Chrism, should be white, while those of the other vessels are of some other colour. The Rubric requires the presence, at the Consecration of the Oils, of twelve Priests, seven Deacons, and seven Subdeacons, besides other ministers, and those officially engaged in the Mass. The Priests, Deacons, and Subdeacons are to wear the vestments of their respective orders In the Sanctuary is prepared for the Consecration of the Oils a table covered with a white linen cloth, near which are placed benches for the Priests and Sacred Ministers assisting at the ceremony. The High Mass is celebrated by the Bishop, and proceeds as usual up to the words 'Per quem hæc omnia' immediately before the Paternoster. The Bishop then de-

* The last stanza is additional.

scends from the Altar, after making his reverence to the Blessed Sacrament there present, and washes his fingers at the Epistle corner, over an empty chalice, of course without receiving the ablution. He then goes to the table already mentioned, and takes his seat at it, with his face towards the Altar. The principal Deacon then says aloud the words, 'Oleum Infirmorum;' whereupon one of the seven Subdeacons goes between two Acolyths to the Sacristy, and returns bearing the vessel of Oil for the Sick, which he delivers into the hands of the Archdeacon, saying the words, 'Oleum Infirmorum.' The Archdeacon then presents the vessel to the Bishop with the same words. The Bishop then *exorcises*, and afterwards blesses, the oil, according to a prescribed form of words. The consecrated oil is then removed, and the Bishop, after washing his hands, returns to the Altar, where he continues the Mass till the Ablutions, receiving with the others that which had remained after the previous washing of his fingers over the chalice. He then adores the Blessed Sacrament reserved for the next day, and returns to his seat at the table for the consecration of the remaining oils. The Archdeacon then asks, as before, for the oil which is to be blessed for the Chrism, and that of the Catechumens; and the Bishop having put incense into the thurible, a procession is formed to the Sacristy, consisting of all the assisting Priests, Deacons, Subdeacons, and other Ministers, and preceded by the thurifer, and the Cross carried by a Subdeacon between two Acolyths with lighted candles. All proceed to the Sacristy, where two Deacons receive the vessels of oil to be consecrated, and return, bearing them under linen humeral veils. They are preceded by a Subdeacon, with the balsam to be infused in the Chrism, and two chanters singing the verses of the hymn, 'O Redemptor,' alternately with the choir. When the procession has returned, the Priests, Deacons, Subdeacons, and others arrange themselves in order; the Priests as coöperators in the consecration, the others as witnesses or assistants. Then the Deacon, bearing the oil for the Chrism, delivers it to the Archdeacon, and he to the Bishop. The Bishop then blesses the balsam. He then mixes a portion of the oil with the balsam. He afterwards breathes upon the oil in the form of a cross; and the same is done by each Priest present in succession. The breathing over objects is a ceremony frequently used in solemn benedictions, and is an imitation of our Blessed Lord's action, as when He breathed upon the Apostles, who immediately received the Holy Ghost. The Bishop then exorcises and blesses the Chrism; after which he sings the Preface, concluding it with words in a low but audible tone of voice. He afterwards mixes the paste of balsam and oil with the rest of the oil, and then salutes, on his knees, the Chrism with the words, 'Hail, holy Chrism!' which he repeats a second and third time, each time in a higher tone of voice, and then kisses the edge of the vessel. The same salutation, with the same ceremonies, is then made by each of the Priests present in succession.

The consecration of the Chrism being ended, the Bishop proceeds to consecrate the oil of the Catechumens with the same ceremonies, excepting that no Preface is sung, and that balsam is not infused into the oil. The two vessels of consecrated oil are then borne back to the Sacristy with the same ceremonies as before, and the Bishop, having washed his hands, returns to the Altar, and concludes the Mass. The holy oils which remain from the preceding year are consumed in the lamp which burns before the Blessed Sacrament, and the newly-consecrated oils are alone used, during the year following, in the various rites into which Unction is introduced, whether as the matter of the Sacrament, or as complementary to it.

It will thus have appeared with what extraordinary

marks of reverence the Church accompanies the Consecration of the Holy Oils. Her practice in this respect is intended to guide both her Priests and people as to the light in which the Holy Oils are to be regarded, and the reverence with which they are to be treated and used. Nor, when we consider, on the one hand, the exalted nature of the purposes to which the Holy Oils are applied, and, on the other, the facility with which irreverence about holy things creeps in, can we wonder that the Church should have invested this act of Benediction with circumstances of such unusual majesty and solemnity.

The several Holy Oils are used on the following occasions: the Chrism, in the ceremonies of Baptism, as well as in the preparation of the Baptismal Water, in Confirmation, at the Consecration of a Bishop, and likewise of Churches, Altars, and Chalices. It is also used in the Consecration of Church Bells. The Oil of the Catechumens is used in the ceremonies of Baptism, in the preparation of the Baptismal Water, at the Ordination of Priests, and the Coronation of Sovereigns. The Oil of the Sick is the sacramental matter of Extreme Unction, and is also used in the blessing of Church Bells.*

The various uses of the Holy Oils, as well as the principal practices in the ceremony of their consecration, are described in the following stanzas:

Our Lord is prodigal of gifts to-day,
    His mercies with His steps harmonious move;
Or if He pause, He pauses to display
    New signs of power, new miracles of love.

Twice, ere the Rite of rites be yet complete,
    Lo, where the mitred Celebrant descends
To bless, with holy words and actions meet,
    The oil of gladness to its destin'd ends!

* The reason appears to be, that the church bell is supposed to be tolled when the soul is passing from the body.

And while each white-rob'd priest in order pays
  Glad homage to the source of health divine,
Our grateful hearts shall echo forth the praise,
  And in the Church's world-wide 'Ave' join.

Hail, holy Oil ![*] thou sweet and sovereign balm!
  Matter of that Last Sacrament whence flow
The sure relief and placid holy calm
  That settle oft on languor's anxious brow;

At whose soft touch and merciful Avaunt
  Death halts abash'd, and drops his ready arms
And Angels haste to guard their favour'd haunt
  From sin's approach, or terror's vain alarms.

Yea, e'en the tones of that heart-piercing bell.
  Whose echoes ring of death, by thee are blest,
And, tun'd by Christian hope, to mourners tell
  Of friends or passed, or passing, to their rest.

Hail, holy Oil ![†] that, ere baptismal streams
  Have blanch'd the marks of sin's deforming trace,
Pour'st on the darken'd heart the twilight gleams
  That pledge the sunshine of converting grace.

Yet nam'd art thou in loftier ministries;
  Strength of the hands that consecrate or bless;
Whose unction health to Priests and Kings supplies
  In duty's need or empire's harrowing stress.

Hail, holy Chrism! which, like the voice from heaven
  That once the Son on Jordan's bank reveal'd,
Art God's own signal of adoption giv'n
  To those whom in His Name the Church hath seal'd;

* The Oil of the Sick.
† The Oil of the Catechumens.

And whom, when rip'ning now for manhood's race,
With sev'nfold strength that Mother's arm endows,
Fain by thine aid the character to trace
Of Christ's own soldier on their youthful brows.

With thee she claims to God each holy place
And vessel wrought for Eucharist sublime,
And nerves the Pontiff with his crowning grace,
And gifts with heav'nward voice the belfry's chime.

Bear off, ye vested guards, your sacred store,
By blessing hallow'd, and with blessings rife;
Whence from a hundred founts the tide shall pour
Whose streams refresh the Church's yearly life.*

The Washing of the Feet.

In Cathedral Churches, or others which may be selected for the purpose, it is customary for the Bishop of each Diocese, or the local Superior, to perform, in the afternoon of Holy Thursday, the ceremony of washing the feet of thirteen poor men, in imitation of the example set and proposed by our Blessed Lord at the Last Supper. The ceremony is as follows: the Bishop, vested in a purple cope, and attended by a Deacon and Subdeacon, vested in white, proceeds from the Sacristy in the usual order to the part of the church appointed for the ceremony. All having made the proper reverences, the Gospel appropriate to the occasion is sung by the Deacon as at High Mass. The Bishop is then divested of his cope, and girded with a linen towel of apron, after which he proceeds to wash the right foot or thirteen poor men seated on a bench, and wipe them with a linen towel, giving an alms to each. The choir in the mean time sing certain prescribed Antiphons. The Washing of the Feet being ended, the Bishop washes

* *Lyra Liturgica:* Holy Thursday.

his hands, and, being revested with a cope, sings the appointed prayer at the Epistle corner of the Altar, after which all retire in the order in which they entered.

VII.

GOOD FRIDAY.

The Office of this day is peculiar, and singularly expressive of its mournful subject. The High Altar and Sanctuary are completely divested of every ornament; and even the Altar-cloth is removed till the Office has begun. The Priest and his Ministers, vested in black,* and preceded by a procession of Clerics, but without Cross, lights, or incense, enter the Sanctuary, where Priest, Deacon, and Subdeacon prostrate at the foot of the Altar, and remain in that posture for a certain space of time, the other attendants all kneeling. During the prostration the Acolyths take the Altar-cloth from the credence-table, bear it over the heads of the Priest and Sacred Ministers, and place it on the Altar. The Master of Ceremonies then removes the Missal from the credence-table to the Epistle side of the Altar. The Priest and Sacred Ministers having gone up to the Altar, pass to the Epistle side, where the Priest reads a short Lesson, which is at the same time sung by a Cleric. The Priest afterwards sings the Collect, and says the Epistle, which is sung by the Subdeacon. The Priest then says the Tract, which is sung by the choir; and towards the close of it three Deacons enter the Sanctuary to sing the Passion, with the same ceremonies as on Palm Sunday, excepting that the Deacons wear black instead of purple stoles and maniples. The Gospel is afterwards sung by the ordinary Deacon, but without lights and incense; neither is the usual Benediction given by the Priest to the Deacon, nor does the Sub-

* The Sacred Ministers wear black folded chasubles; or, at any rate, not dalmatic and tunic.

deacon carry the Book of the Gospel for the Priest to kiss the first words of the text.

The Gospel over, the Priest proceeds to sing, at the Epistle corner of the Altar, the prayers for different estates of men, which will be found in the Missal. Each prayer is preceded by an invitation to pray for those who are the objects of it; and this invitation is followed by one made by the Deacon to bend the knee, after which the Subdeacon responds 'Arise.' There is, however, one exception to this latter address, which is in the case of the Prayer for the Jews; and the reason assigned for this exception is, that the Church refuses to perform in their regard an action which they desecrated by employing it in mockery of our Blessed Lord during the time of His Passion.

The prayers over, the Master of Ceremonies takes down the Crucifix from its place above the Altar, and the Priest, going to the Epistle corner, uncovers the top of the Cross, and, exhibiting it to the people, sings in a low tone the words 'Ecce lignum Crucis,' &c. &c., which will be found in the Missal, and which are continued by some of the choir, all kneeling at the words 'Venite adoremus;' the Priest then ascends the step, and, standing at the Epistle corner of the Altar, uncovers the right arm of the figure, and exhibits it as before, singing the same words in a somewhat higher tone, which the choir continues as before. He then advances to the middle of the Altar, where he uncovers and exhibits the whole figure, singing the same words in a still higher tone. At the same moment all the Crosses in the church are uncovered. The Crucifix is then placed by the Deacon on a cushion at the foot of the Altar for the adoration of the Clergy and people. It is first adored by the Priest and Sacred Ministers, who approach it without their exterior vestments and without shoes. The Clergy follow, and then the people. Those who approach the Cross go down three times on their knees;

the last time at the foot of the Cross itself. They salute the feet, and, after once more kneeling, retire. In some churches it is customary to place a dish by the side of the Cross for the reception of alms. Where the numbers in the church are large, another Cross may be presented for adoration by a Priest in some convenient part of the church. While the Adoration of the Cross is going on, the choir sings the Reproaches, which will be found in the Missal; and the Priest and his Ministers say them, with all else which is prescribed, at the Sedilia.

The Adoration of the Cross being over, the Deacon goes, accompanied by the Master of Ceremonies, to remove it and replace it over the Altar. The six large candles of the Altar having been lighted, and the corporal spread on the Altar, a procession is formed, preceded by thurifers with their thuribles, but without incense, and by the Parochial Cross, borne between Acolyths with lighted candles, and advances to the Altar of Repose. Having arrived there, the Deacon unlocks the Ark containing the Blessed Sacrament, and opening the door of it, descends to assist the Priest in placing incense in the thurible. At the same time lighted tapers are given to the choir and attendants. The Priest having incensed the Blessed Sacrament, the Deacon takes It down and places It in the hands of the Priest, who receives It on his knees. It is then borne under the canopy in procession to the High Altar, the choir singing the hymn 'Vexilla Regis.' On reaching the High Altar, the Priest, having placed the chalice containing the Blessed Sacrament on the Altar, proceeds to incense It on both his knees. The chalice is then divested of the veil, and the Sacred Host contained within it transferred to the paten; after which wine and water are poured into the chalice, and the usual incensation takes place, except that the Priest himself is not incensed. He then washes his fingers as usual, and going to the middle of the Altar says the 'Orate, fratres;' but on account of the presence of the Blessed Sacrament without turning completely round and without receiving the usual response. He then sings the Paternoster; after which he elevates the Sacred Host for adoration, and then divides It, and places a portion in the chalice as usual. He afterwards receives the Sacred Host, saying, however, before Communion the last of the three preparatory prayers only. He afterwards receives the contents of the chalice, and having taken the ablutions, makes over the chalice to the Subdeacon to be properly arranged, and retires from the Altar without saying any other words. The choir remains to sing the Vespers, as on the preceding day, and the Altar is afterwards stripped.

The purpose of the Church in this marvellously beautiful Office is to represent the desolation consequent on the death of her Lord. The Office may be said to be at once most irregular and most orderly. It consists in a series of detached actions, and terminates in one which has the semblance without the reality of a Mass. It is called the Mass of the Presanctified, consisting as it does merely in the consumption of the preconsecrated Host, with so much of the usual Office of the Mass only as bears upon that act, and is necessary to invest it with a becoming dignity. But on the day when the Church is absorbed in the contemplation of the Sacrifice of the Cross, she suspends for once her daily Oblation of that Sacrifice in the form in which her divine Lord has commanded her to commemorate, represent, and apply it.

In Rome, and in some churches in this country, the Devotion called the 'Three Hours' is preached on Good Friday in memory of the three hours during which our Lord hung upon the Cross. It consists of brief meditative discourses on the 'Seven Words,' or sayings, of our Blessed Lord on the Cross, which are as follows: 1. 'Father, forgive them, for they know not what they do.' 2. 'To-day thou shalt be with Me in Paradise.'

3. 'Mother, behold thy son;—son, behold thy Mother.' 4. 'My God, My God, why hast Thou forsaken Me?' 5. 'I thirst.' 6. 'It is consummated.' 7. 'Father, into Thy hands I commend My spirit.' It is usual to occupy the interval between the discourses with pieces of illustrative music, to which the rule relating to the exclusion of instruments does not apply, as this devotion is no part of the Church Office.

VIII.

HOLY SATURDAY.

Good Friday is a day of desolation. Even the Blessed Sacrament, after the Mass of the Presanctified has been celebrated, disappears from the church, or is at all events reserved in some chapel which is shut out from general observation. The Crucifixes are indeed uncovered, but the Altars remain divested of every kind of ornament, and even of their usual covering. The Tenebræ Office is recited towards evening for the last time. The Psalms are shorter than on the preceding evenings, and their character somewhat different. Instead of bringing into prominence the sufferings and the indignities of the Passion, their prevailing sentiment is that of *rest*, since the Passion is now over, and the Church wishes to bring before the mind the transactions of that solemn interval between the ninth hour, or three o'clock, on the Friday, when our Lord expired, and the dawn of the third day, when He arose from the dead. It is therefore not unusual to occupy the evening of this day with devotions in honour of our Lady of Dolours, who stands out in strong prominence during this interval. In some foreign countries there are processions commemorative of the Burial of our Lord on the evening of Good Friday.

On the morning of Holy Saturday, a slight change is perceptible in the aspect of the church. The High

Altar is once more vested in purple; and such preparations for the High Mass as cannot be expedited in the short time which elapses between the end of the Office proper to Holy Saturday and the beginning of Mass are made at an earlier hour. At the entrance of the church or, should the weather permit, on the outside of it preparations are made for the Benediction of the new fire. The Baptistery is also prepared with all that is necessary for the Benediction of the Font, and presents a festive appearance. In addition to the other arrangements of the Sanctuary, the Paschal Candle is placed at the Gospel side of the Altar on its stand, and near it a desk for the use of the Deacon who is to sing the form of blessing prescribed by the Church. This form, from the word with which it commences, is called the 'Exultet.'

At the appointed hour, the Priest and Sacred Ministers advance in procession, preceded by the Parochial Cross, and by Clerks, bearing what is necessary for the ceremony at the entrance of the church. When all have arrived at the place appointed for the blessing of the new fire, the Priest recites the preparatory prayer, and blesses the fire, which should be struck from a flint. He afterwards blesses the incense kindled from the new fire, and then the five large grains of it which are afterwards to be inserted in the Paschal Candle. This over, the Deacon exchanges the purple vestment proper to the ceremony of blessing the fire for white, and then receives into his hand a rod, at the extremity of which are three candles. The procession then advances into the church, and, at the entrance of it, the Deacon lights from the new fire one of the three candles on the rod, and sings, in a low key, the words 'Lumen Christi,' that is, the Light of Christ. He is answered by the choir, 'Deo gratias,' 'Thanks be to God.' At these words all go down on their knees, except the Cross-bearer. The procession then advances, and, when it has reached the middle of the church, it halts, and the Deacon sings the same words in a higher tone, with the same ceremonies. He sings them for the third time when the procession reaches the Sanctuary, and then lights the last of the three candles on the triple candlestick.

The object of these beautiful ceremonies seems to be, on the one hand, to remind us that the renewal of all nature is one of the effects of the Resurrection of our Lord; and, on the other, to console us by suggesting that Christ, the Light of the World, has been only obscured, and is not extinguished by death. This latter thought is brought out still more by the Benediction of the Paschal Candle which follows; for the Paschal Candle, remaining in the church, as it does, from Holy Saturday till Ascension-day, is evidently intended to symbolise the glorified presence of our Lord during the forty days of His sojourn on earth after His Resurrection.

When the procession has reached the Sanctuary, the officiating Priest goes to the Epistle corner of the Altar, while the Deacon who is to bless the Paschal Candle receives the Book of the Gospel, and, after obtaining the benediction of the Priest, goes to the desk to sing the 'Præconium,' or announcement of the approach of Easter. At certain parts of this magnificent address he pauses: first, to insert the five grains of incense into the Paschal Candle; secondly, to light the Paschal Candle from the triple candle previously mentioned; and thirdly, to allow time for lighting the lamps before the High Altar and the other Altars of the church, which now begins to present a more jubilant appearance. When the blessing of the Paschal Candle is concluded, the Deacon re-assumes the purple vestments, and joins the Priest at the Altar, together with the Subdeacon. The Priest then reads in a low tone of voice the twelve Prophecies, or Lessons, of the Old Testament, which are at the same time sung by a cleric in the choir; and at the conclusion of each Lesson the Priest sings a Collect, preceded by '*Oremus*,' to which the Deacon and Subdeacon respectively answer, 'Flectamus genua' ('Let us bend the knee'), and 'Levate' ('Arise'); and the summons, in each case, is obeyed by the choir and people. At the last of the twelve lessons, which describes Nabuchodonosor's act of idolatry, the invitation to kneel is not given, as if in abhorrence of that profane decree. After three of the Prophecies, short canticles from the Old Testament are sung. The intention of the Church in appointing the recitation of these ancient prophecies appears to have been originally that of providing instruction for the catechumens, who used to receive baptism on this day.

When the Prophecies are concluded, the Priest and his Ministers go in procession to bless the Baptismal Font. The Paschal Candle is borne at the head of the procession before the Cross. During the procession the choir sings the beautiful words of the psalm, 'As the hart panteth after the fountains,' &c. When the Priest reaches the Baptistery he sings at the entrance the prescribed prayer, after which he goes to the Font and sings that wonderful Preface in which the great doctrine of Regeneration in baptism is so copiously illustrated by the types of the Old Law, and the words of our Blessed Lord. At certain parts of the Preface he pauses to perform the actions prescribed for the blessing of the water, one of which is the triple immersion of the Paschal Candle, and finally infuses into it, first, the holy Oil of the Catechumens; secondly, the holy Chrism; and lastly, both of these holy Oils together. Previously to the infusion of the Oils, the people are sprinkled by one of the Priests present with the blessed water. The ceremony being concluded, and the officiating Priest having purified his hands from the portions of the holy Oils which may have adhered to them, the procession returns to the High Altar. As soon as it leaves the Baptistery, or (according to the practice of some churches) when it reaches the High Altar, the chanters begin the Litanies of the Saints, all the petitions of which, on this occasion only, are recited entire both by the chanters and respondents. When the officiating Priest and his Ministers reach the Altar, they prostrate at its foot, and remain in that posture till the word 'Peccatores' in the Litanies has been uttered, the other attendants all kneeling.* At the word 'Peccatores,' the Priest and Sacred Ministers rise and go to the sacristy, while the rest remain to continue the Litanies. The Altar is then divested of the emblems of mourning, and adorned with all the tokens of joy and festivity which the brief interval admits. The Priest and Sacred Ministers then re-enter the church in the richest vestments of white or gold, preceded by the acolyths with lighted candles and the other attendants. The choir then sings the 'Kyrie eleison,' at the end of the Litanies, to serve as the beginning of the Mass. The Celebrant, having recited the several portions of the Mass to the end of the Kyrie, and incensed the Altar as usual, intones the 'Gloria in excelsis.' As soon as he has pronounced those words, the interior and exterior bells of the church are rung, the organ strikes up, and continues to play, and the bells to ring, whilst the Celebrant recites the 'Gloria.' When he has concluded it, the Sanctuary bell ceases, but the outer bells of the church may continue to ring till the music of the 'Gloria' is ended. At Rome, and in some Catholic countries, a salvo of artillery is fired at the announcement of the 'Gloria.' At the same moment all pictures and images in the church are divested of their mournful drapery. When the Collect and

* This may be a suitable occasion for observing, that *prostration* is always, according to the rule of the Church, a posture of personal humiliation, and not adoration. Hence it is incorrect to prostrate at Benediction or other Expositions of the Most Holy Sacrament.

Epistle have been sung, the Celebrant gives out thrice, and each time in a higher pitch, the word Alleluia, which is taken up in the same tones by the choir. When a Bishop celebrates this Mass, he is addressed, before giving out the Alleluia, in words of which the following is a translation: 'Most Reverend Father, I announce to you a great joy, which is, Alleluia.' The Mass then proceeds to the end of the Gospel, after which the Celebrant, omitting the Credo, proceeds to the Offertory, and continues, as usual, to the words 'Pax Domini;' the 'Agnus Dei' is omitted, and the kiss of peace not given, perhaps because the Church now, as on Holy Thursday, avoids any reference to an act of salutation which was desecrated by the Traitor. After the Celebrant has received the Holy Communion, and administered it to any who may desire to communicate, and when he has taken the usual ablutions, the Vespers of the day are sung, beginning with the short Psalm, 'Laudate Dominum omnes gentes' (cxvi.). The Magnificat is then sung with its proper antiphon, and the Altar, Priest, and Choir incensed as usual. At the end of the Mass, 'Ite missa est' is sung, with the addition of two Alleluias, to a tone peculiar to Easter week.

IX.

PASCHAL-TIDE.

The more immediate and joyous celebration of Easter is confined to the first week, which presents some special features as compared even with the rest of Paschaltide. One of these is the addition of two Alleluias to the 'Ite missa est' at Mass, and to the 'Benedicamus Domino' of Lauds and Vespers, as well as to the response following both. Another is the Sequence in the Mass 'Victimæ Paschali,' and the Gradual 'Hæc dies,' which verse is also introduced throughout 'the Offices' of the week, in the place of the usual capitulum and hymn.

The peculiarities of the Paschal-time are the following: 1. The more frequent use of Alleluias in the Mass and Office. 2. The substitution of the 'Vidi aquam' for the 'Asperges.' 3. The use of the 'Regina Cœli' at the end of Lauds and Complin, and the practice of standing as a token of alacrity and joy during the recitation of this hymn, even on week-days, when it is customary to kneel at the Hymn of the Blessed Virgin at the other three seasons of the year. 4. The use of a special Mass and Office for Martyrs. 5. The presence of the Paschal Candle in the Sanctuary till the Gospel in the High Mass of Ascension-day; after which it is extinguished and removed. The Paschal Candle is lighted at all solemn Offices, except at High Masses of the Dead, and except also (unless the contrary usage prevails) at the High Mass which follows the Litanies on the Feast of St. Mark and the Rogation-days. 6. The recitation of the Litanies of the Saints on St. Mark's Day (April 25), even when the celebration of that feast is transferred, and on the three Rogation-days immediately preceding the Feast of the Ascension.

PART IV.

Devotional Practices of the Church.

I.

INDULGENCES.

This little work would be incomplete if I did not prefix to this portion of the subject a few words on the subject of Indulgences. An Indulgence is a remission of the temporal penalty of sins, the eternal penalty of which is remitted in the Sacrament of Penance. This doctrine on the true nature of Indulgences must always be borne in mind as a reply to the objections of heretics and ignorant persons, and as an explanation of any language which may be employed by Catholics in reference to them. A Plenary Indulgence is usually interpreted to mean a remission of the whole temporal penalty due to sin; a partial Indulgence is the remission of such a portion of that penalty as corresponds with the periods of penance appointed in the early ages. The usual conditions of a Plenary Indulgence are, the worthy reception of the Sacraments of Penance and the Blessed Eucharist, and prayers for the intentions of the Sovereign Pontiff—that is to say, peace and concord among Christian princes, the extirpation of heresy, and the exaltation of our holy Mother the Church. For gaining a partial Indulgence the reception of the fore-mentioned Sacraments is not necessary; but no Indulgence can be gained except by such Christians as are in a state of grace—*i.e.* free from mortal sin; and it is the more common opinion of spiritual writers, that Plenary Indulgences require, in order to gain them, an amount of perfection in the mode of performing their conditions which is by no means common. Devout and humble Catholics, however, who feel the weight of their sins, and the insufficiency of their penance, will always be glad to embrace the opportunity of gaining such spiritual favours to the best of their ability. Plenary Indulgences, applicable to the souls in Purgatory, can either be gained by the person who performs their conditions for him or herself, or can be applied to the departed souls in general, or to any particular soul whose benefit is desired, but cannot be gained vicariously for another living person. When applied for the benefit of the dead, they are said, in the language of theology, to avail 'by way of suffrage,' or in other words, to be offered to God in order to be applied according to His sovereign

Will; but with a prayer that He would be pleased to apply them according to the special intention of the person who so offers them. It is necessary towards gaining an Indulgence to have at least the intention of gaining it; but this intention need not be formed on each particular occasion, provided it be renewed from time to time, so as to be an habitual disposition of the mind. It is the pious practice of many Catholics to form every morning the intention of gaining all the Indulgences which may be attached to practices they may perform during the day.

II.

THE STATIONS OF THE CROSS.

The Devotion of the Stations is a pious method of commemorating the Passion of our Blessed Saviour. It has been already stated that among the objects which are most commonly met with in the interior of our churches, are the fourteen representations of our Lord's sorrowful progress to Calvary, and of His Crucifixion, with the events immediately subsequent to it. The Devotion of the Stations consists in visiting each of these pictures in their proper order, beginning with the first, which represents our Lord's Condemnation, and ending with the fourteenth, which represents His Burial. The Stations are as follows: 1. Our Lord is condemned to death. 2. He takes up the Cross. 3. He falls the first time. 4. He meets His Most Holy Mother. 5. He is assisted in bearing His Cross by Simon of Cyrene. 6. He is met by St. Veronica. 7. He falls a second time. 8. He meets the holy women of Jerusalem. 9. He falls the third time. 10. He is stripped of His garments, and has gall given Him to drink. 11. He is nailed to the Cross. 12. He dies on the Cross. 13. He is taken down from the Cross. 14. He is buried.

When the Devotion of the Stations is publicly performed, the Priest, vested in surplice and purple stole, preceded by the Cross between acolyths bearing lighted candles, goes to one of the Altars, and there recites the Act of Contrition with the people. He afterwards proceeds to the different Stations in succession, the people singing on the way from one Station to another a stanza of the 'Stabat Mater,' or other appropriate hymn. When the Priest comes to each Station, he first says the versicle, 'We adore Thee, O Christ, and we praise Thee,' and is answered, 'Because by Thy holy Cross Thou hast redeemed the world;' then he reads a short meditation on the subject before him, and afterwards recites the 'Our Father,' the 'Hail Mary,' and 'Glory be to the Father.' The people genuflect at the versicle, stand at the meditation, and kneel at the prayers. When all the Stations have been visited, the Priest returns to the Altar, says some prayers for the intentions of the Pope, and blesses the people with the Crucifix.

The Stations are often made privately by devout persons. Very ample Indulgences have been attached to this pious practice, but for the gaining of these it is necessary that all the Stations should be visited, by going from one to another, or at least, where this cannot be done, by turning the body in the direction of each. The Pope, and those to whom his Holiness may be pleased to impart the same privilege, have power to bless Crosses with annexation of these Indulgences for the use of devout persons who, whether by illness, imprisonment, or any unavoidable hindrance, are prevented from making the Stations of the Cross in a church or other sacred place.

The erection of the Stations in a church, cemetery, or elsewhere, requires a faculty, or permission from authority. The devotion grew out of the ancient practice of visiting the Holy Places in Palestine, and enjoys the benefit of the same Indulgences as belonged to the pilgrimages of which it forms the modern substitute.

III.

THE ANGELUS.

The Angelus is an indulgenced practice of devotion to be performed three times a day, at the sound of a bell which is rung from the steeple of all Catholic churches. Where no church with a bell is near, the notice for the Angelus may be given by a bell in a house. The usual hours for ringing the Angelus are six in the morning, twelve at noon, and six in the evening; but at Rome, the morning and evening hours are regulated by the rising and setting of the sun. The devotion consists in the recitation of three 'Hail Maries' (each preceded by a versicle and response), at the close of which is said the prayer of the Blessed Virgin which follows the hymn proper to Advent. The Devotion of the Angelus is a repeated commemoration of the Incarnation of our Lord, and of the sacred Maternity of the Blessed Virgin. There is a separate Indulgence for adding three 'Gloria Patris' to the Angelus.

During Paschal-tide it is customary to say the 'Regina Cœli' instead of the Angelus. The Regina Cœli is always said standing; the Angelus kneeling, except on Sundays.

It is also prescribed that a bell should be rung in commemoration of the dead one hour after the evening Angelus, and another on Fridays in commemoration of our Lord's Death three hours before it. But these practices are not as yet commonly introduced into England.

IV.

THE ROSARY.

The Rosary is a popular devotion of the Church, first used by Saint Dominic in combating the heresies of his time. It consists of fifteen meditations upon Mysteries of the Faith, during each of which are recited one Our Father, ten Hail Maries, and one Gloria Patri. The fifteen Mysteries are divided into three portions, consisting of five each, and called respectively the Joyful, the Sorrowful, and the Glorious Mysteries. When these portions are recited separately, the Joyful are appointed for Mondays and Thursdays, the Sorrowful for Tuesdays and Fridays, and the Glorious for Wednesdays and Saturdays. The Joyful Mysteries may also be said on the Sundays beginning with the first Sunday in Advent and ending on the last Sunday before Lent: the Sorrowful Mysteries on the Sundays in Lent; and the Glorious Mysteries between Easter and Advent. The Joyful Mysteries are as follows: 1. the Annunciation; 2. the Visitation; 3. the Nativity; 4. the Purification; 5. the Finding of the Child Jesus in the Temple. The Sorrowful Mysteries are: 1. the Agony in the Garden; 2. the Scourging; 3. the Crowning with thorns; 4. the Carrying of the Cross; 5. the Crucifixion. The Glorious are: 1. the Resurrection; 2. the Ascension; 3. the Descent of the Holy Spirit; 4. the Assumption of the Blessed Virgin; 5. the Coronation of the Blessed Virgin. The Rosary is said upon a string of beads, called by the same name, and so arranged as to admit of one 'I believe' and three 'Gloria Patris' being said at the beginning of each division or set of five Mysteries. These introductory prayers, however, form no part of the Rosary properly so called, which consists of one 'Our Father,' ten 'Hail Maries,' and one 'Gloria Patri' for each Mystery. It is usual, when the Rosary is said in public, to call the several Mysteries to mind by a few preliminary words. When the Rosary is said with others, the person saying it (who need not be even a Cleric) recites half of each prayer, the rest reciting the other half, and beginning the prayers alternately with him, so that every other time he will recite the second half of the prayer.

V.

THE MONTH OF MARY.

According to the universal practice of the Church, the month of May is dedicated to the honour of the Blessed Virgin, and pious persons are in the habit of marking each day of it by some special devotion to her. These devotions are frequently accompanied by hymns or canticles in the vernacular. A partial Indulgence can be gained on each day of the month by those who observe this practice, whether in public or in private, and a Plenary Indulgence on the usual conditions by those who follow it every day. The Litany of Loreto is frequently sung in procession during the month of Mary, as well as at other times. It is sung on the knees as far as the words 'Sancta Maria,' at which the procession begins to move; on its return to the Altar, the 'Agnus Dei' is sung, followed by the usual versicle and response, and the prayer, which is always that beginning 'Concede nos,' excepting during Advent and Christmas, when the prayers proper to those seasons are substituted. An image of our Lady is often borne in these processions.

VI.

OTHER POPULAR DEVOTIONS.

There are many public Devotions approved by the Church, besides those already mentioned; but as they do not involve any special forms in their use, they do not require particular notice in this work. Among those which are most general may be mentioned the Devotions to the Blessed Sacrament, to the Sacred Heart of Jesus, to His Most Precious Blood, to His Five Wounds, to the Holy and Immaculate Heart of Mary, and to the Seven Dolours.

The reader is directed to the English translation of the Roman *Raccolta* (published by Messrs. Burns and Oates) for the most approved Catholic Devotions, with the Indulgences attached to the use of them by successive Sovereign Pontiffs.

APPENDIX.

Occasional Offices of the Church.

I.

BAPTISM OF INFANTS.

INFANTS are always baptised in the church of the parochial district in which they are born, excepting in the case of dangerous illness, or by the special permission of the Bishop. Parents are admonished to bring their children to the church for Baptism as soon as possible after their birth, and incur a grave responsibility by the neglect of this rule. Parents cannot themselves be sponsors. The public ceremonies of Baptism are not essential to the Sacrament, which requires only the use of the proper matter and form of words, which must both be employed at one and the same time; but, when private Baptism has been administered without the ceremonies, the child, should it live, ought to be brought to the church, in order that so much of the rite as had been necessarily omitted may be supplied.

The sponsors are first asked, in the name of the child, what they seek at the hands of the Church, and are instructed that Faith, in order to lead to eternal life, must be accompanied by Obedience to the Commandments. The Priest then breathes upon the infant, and having expelled from it the unclean Spirit, makes on its forehead and breast the sign of the Cross. After two preliminary prayers, he places salt, previously exorcised and blessed, in the mouth of the child, saying, '*N.* Receive the salt of wisdom; may it be a propitiation to thee unto life eternal! Peace be with thee.—*R.* And with thy spirit!' The Evil Spirit, which in consequence of Original Sin still possesses the soul, is afterwards exorcised in the name of the Most Holy Trinity, and commanded not to violate the holy sign of the Cross, which the Priest then forms on the forehead of the child. After a prayer for spiritual illumination, the Priest, laying the end of his stole on the child, conducts it, with the sponsors, from the door of the church, at which the earlier portion of the rite is performed, to the Baptistery, saying on the way, with the sponsors, the Creed and Our Father. When the Priest has reached the Baptistery, he again exorcises the Evil Spirit from the child, which remains outside in the arms of its sponsor; the Priest next touches the ears and nostrils of the child with spittle, in accordance with the practice of our Lord, saying the word 'Ephpheta,' that is, Be opened; and adds, as he touches the nostrils, 'In the odour of sweetness.' He then requires the sponsors, in the name of the child, to renounce Satan, with all his works and pomps; after which he anoints the child on the breast, and between the shoulders, with the Holy Oil of the Catechumens. He then exchanges the purple stole, which he had hitherto worn, for a white one, and interrogates the child, in the person of its sponsors, on the chief articles of the Creed, concluding with the question, 'Wilt thou be baptised?' whereby the Church signifies that Baptism is a voluntary act. This question having been answered in the affirmative, the child is brought to the Font, where the Priest baptises it by pouring the baptismal water three times on its head, taking care that the water touches the flesh of the child, and not its hair only. He says, while pouring the water, '*N.* I baptise thee in the name of the Father, and of the Son, and of the Holy Ghost, Amen;' which words are said in Latin, but have the same effect when used in any other language. The Priest afterwards anoints the child on the crown of the head with the Holy Chrism. He then places on the child the white garment, emblematic of innocence, accompanying the act with the following beautiful words: 'Receive this white garment, and see thou carry it without stain before the Judgment Seat of our Lord Jesus Christ, that thou mayest have eternal life. Amen.' Finally, he places in the right hands of the sponsors a lighted candle, emblematic of spiritual illumination, saying, 'Receive this burning light, and keep thy Baptism so as to be without blame. Keep the commandments of God; that, when the Lord shall come to the nuptials, thou mayest meet Him in the company of all the Saints in the Heavenly Court, and have eternal life, and live for ever and ever. Amen.' He then dismisses the child with the words, 'Go in peace, and the Lord be with thee.'

Private Baptism may be administered by any one, in case of necessity, when the attendance of a Priest cannot be obtained. When there is a choice of persons to administer it, a cleric is to be preferred to a lay-person, a Catholic to a Protestant. In cases of extreme necessity even the parent of the child is allowed to baptise it. All that is necessary as regards *intention* is, that the baptiser should seriously mean to do what the Church intends. As to the validity of the act itself, it is necessary that the baptiser should use natural water, that this water should flow on the flesh of the child, and that the baptiser, *at the time of pouring the water*, should address the child in the following words: 'I baptise thee in the name of the Father, and of the Son, and of the Holy Ghost. Amen.' The neglect of any of these instructions would render the Baptism invalid, or at any rate doubtful; and, unless it can be certified to the Priest that all has been rightly done, he will have either to re-baptise the child unconditionally, or to baptise it under the condition, 'if thou art not baptised,' accordingly as he shall judge the previous act to be either positively invalid, or not certainly valid. It is the rule of the Church in this country to baptise all converts conditionally, unless it can be proved to the satisfaction of the Priest who receives them that they are certainly baptised already. The reason of this rule is, not that the Church doubts the validity of Baptism administered out of her pale, where the requisite conditions of that Sacrament have been duly observed, but that she desires to guard her members, in a matter of such extreme importance, from the possible effects of a negligence formerly very common, and still apt to occur where the Sacrament of Baptism is not sufficiently appreciated.

II.

THE BAPTISM OF ADULTS.

The Baptism of Adults is properly an Episcopal ceremony, but is often performed by a Priest, to whom the Bishop of the Diocese delegates the necessary power. It is a rite of far more solemn and complex character than the Baptism of infants, and the administration of it is preceded by the recitation of psalms and prayers at the Altar. The Catechumen takes his or her place with the sponsors outside the church, whither the Bishop or Priest who is to administer the rite proceeds, after having said the preliminary portion of it. He begins by asking the Catechumen to give his or her name, and all answers made by the Sponsors at the Baptism of infants are made at that of adults by the Catechumen, with this difference, that the renunciation of Satan, and the profession of faith, which, in the case of infants, take place at the Font only, in the case of adults are made also at the beginning of the rite. The Catechumen is afterwards exorcised with especial reference to the state of darkness out of which he or she is called; whether it be Heathenism, Judaism, Mahometanism, or Heresy. The Catechumen is then signed with the sign of the Cross on the various senses, on the breast and shoulders, and finally on the whole person. Other exorcisms follow; and one of the most striking parts of the ceremony is that in which the Sponsor is instructed to sign the Catechumen with the sign of the Cross, and the latter to recite the Paternoster on bended knee. This is done more than once, and the Catechumen is again exorcised. At length, the Catechumen is introduced into the church, and prostrates at the entrance. He or she afterwards rises, and the Bishop or Priest, placing his hand on the Catechumen's head, recites with him or her the Creed and Paternoster, and afterwards, again placing his hand on the Catechumen's head, once more pronounces a prayer of exorcism. All have now come to the Font, where the same ceremonies take place as have already been described in the case of infant baptism, except that, as has been before mentioned, the questions are answered, not by the Sponsors, but by the Catechumen. To give additional solemnity to the rite, the Bishop or Priest will probably officiate in a cope, which will be of purple colour till the Catechumen has been anointed with the Baptismal Oil, and afterwards of white. It would also be quite in accordance with the intention of the Church, and add to the impressiveness of the rite, that the Catechumen should not merely have the white garment laid upon him or her, as in the case of infants, but be invested with it in the place of some other outer garment, and so return, wearing the white robe of innocence, with lighted candle in hand, into the church, and there either hear Mass, or at least adore the Blessed Sacrament.

III.

THE PUBLIC RECEPTION OF A CONVERT.

It is not necessary that converts to the Church should make their profession and be received in public; but where circumstances render the public reception desirable, it takes place according to a prescribed rule. The Convert, having already received conditional baptism, is introduced into the church and kneels at the foot of the Altar. The Priest then enters vested in surplice and stole, or, if he so please, in cope of purple colour, and, kneeling at the Altar, proceeds to recite with his attendants the hymn 'Veni, Creator,' which, for the sake of greater solemnity, may be sung in choir. The appropriate versicle, response, and prayer having been said or sung, the Priest takes his seat, and, with head covered, recites, alternately with his ministers, on behalf of the Convert, the Psalm 'Miserere,' which might, as I suppose, like the hymn, be chanted in choir. The 'Miserere' being concluded, the Priest takes off his biretta, rises, and recites the Kyrie eleïson, Paternoster, and the usual versicles, to which the proper responses are made. He then recites the prayers for the pardon of the Convert, who thereupon reads the Profession of Faith in the Creed of Pope Pius; after which the Confiteor is recited by the Deacon, or other Minister on behalf of the Convert, and the Priest follows it with the usual prayers for the Divine mercy. He then, without rising, and with head covered, pronounces, in his judicial capacity, the absolution of the Convert from the sentence of excommunication incurred by heresy, restoring him or her to the benefit of the Sacraments and to the Communion of Holy Church. The 'Te Deum' is then sung or said with the proper versicles and prayer, the Priest having previously exchanged the purple stole (and cope, if he have worn one) for white.

N.B.—The rubric of the Ritual does not specify the use of a cope; but analogy, I suppose, would allow it in certain cases; and, as the earlier portion of the rite is penitential, and the conclusion joyful, the colour should be changed, as in Baptism.

IV.

CONFIRMATION.

The ordinary minister of the Sacrament of Confirmation is a Bishop, although the power is, in certain extreme cases, delegated to those who have not received episcopal consecration. The rubric provides that this Sacrament shall be received fasting; but this rule has fallen (at least in England) into disuse, probably on account of the lateness of the hour at which Confirmation is generally given. The ceremonies are as follow:

The Bishop, vested in a white cope, and wearing the mitre, proceeds with his attendants to the Altar, where, the mitre being removed, he stands with his face towards the persons who are to be confirmed, and with hands joined before his breast, says the words, 'May the Holy Spirit come down upon you, and the virtue of the Most High preserve you.' Then, after the usual prefatory words, he extends his hands towards the persons to be confirmed, and prays for the Seven Gifts of the Holy Ghost in their order. He then administers the Sacrament to each several person (kneeling before him) in the following manner: He anoints the forehead with the Chrism in the form of a cross, addressing each by the name of the Saint who has been chosen as a Patron or Patroness, and saying, 'N., I sign thee with the sign of the Cross, and confirm thee with the Chrism of Salvation, in the name of the Father, and of the Son, and of the Holy Ghost. Amen.' While pronouncing the latter words, he makes the sign of the Cross, with his hand towards the person whom he is confirming. Finally, he touches the left cheek with his hand, saying 'Peace be with thee.' The holy oil is then removed from the forehead with cotton wool, or, as is the more rubrical practice followed in some Catholic countries, the forehead is bound with a linen bandage till the oil is absorbed. The ceremony of touching the cheek is supposed to symbolise the opposition which the youthful soldier of Christ must expect from the world; and the words 'Peace be with thee' to denote the promised consolation of the Gospel and of the Paraclete. When all have been confirmed, a short verse is sung by the choir, after which the Bishop recites a prayer for the confirmed, still kneeling before him, and says the words 'Lo, thus shall the man be blessed that feareth the Lord.' He then dismisses the confirmed persons with a benediction.

V.

MATRIMONY.

Persons who intend to enter the holy state of Matrimony should present themselves before the Priest who is to celebrate the marriage at least three weeks before the day on which they wish it to take place, in order to ascertain if there be any impediment to the marriage, and receive such instructions as may be necessary. The most usual impediments to marriage, which require a dispensation for their removal, are such as arise out of some relationship between the parties, or from difference of religion. It does not, however, fall within the scope of the present work to deal with this part of the subject.

It is most in accordance with the intention of the Church that Mass should be celebrated at the time of marriage; but this condition is not indispensable, and, in our own country, is too frequently omitted. The Church has provided, among her *Votive Masses* for special occasions, one of singular beauty for the celebration of marriage. This Mass may be said or sung on any ordinary feast, even though a *double,* provided it be not a festival of the second class, and when a festival of that or any higher degree occurs on the day of the marriage, those portions of the proper Mass of Marriage which are immediately connected with the celebration of the rite are allowed to be introduced into the Mass of the festival.

The Bride and Bridegroom, with their friends, having taken their places near the Altar (the bridegroom standing at the right hand of the bride), the Priest vested in surplice and white stole (over which he may wear a white or gold cope) proceeds with his attendants to the Altar, where, after a short preliminary prayer, he turns to the bride and bridegroom, interrogates them each as to their consent, and afterwards proposes to them the form of words by which that consent is mutually expressed. He then joins their hands in marriage, in the name of the Most Blessed Trinity, and afterwards sprinkles them with holy water. He next requires the bridegroom to place in a salver the ring, and some pieces of gold and silver coin, to be given into the hands of the bride. He then blesses the ring, sprinkles it with holy water, and gives it into the hand of the bridegroom, instructing him to say the words in which he declares that he weds the bride with that ring, and makes over to her the gold and silver as a pledge of his fidelity, 'in the name of the Father, and of the Son, and of the Holy Ghost. Amen.' As the bridegroom names the 'Father,' he touches the thumb of the bride's left hand with the ring, her forefinger as he names the 'Son,' the next finger as he names the 'Holy Ghost,' and places it on her fourth finger as he says the word 'Amen.' The Priest then turns to the Altar, and says certain versicles with the Kyrie and Paternoster, after which, if Mass be celebrated, he puts on the sacerdotal vestments (which will be white, unless the Mass, being of one of the higher festivals, should require red), and begins the Mass. It proceeds as usual to the Paternoster, at the end of which he goes to the Epistle corner of the Altar, where he pronounces the benediction of the bride, if it be her first marriage; he then returns to the middle of the Altar, and proceeds with the Mass, at which it is very usual for the bride and bridegroom to receive the Holy Communion. Immediately before the benediction of the people at the end of the Mass, the Priest again turns round, and pronounces a benediction on the newly-married pair kneeling before him. It is also customary for him to address to them some words of exhortation, both before and after the marriage-rite. If Mass be not celebrated, the Priest pronounces the two benedictions at the end of the ceremony.

The law of this country requires that the civil registrar shall be present at all Catholic marriages, and that the bride and bridegroom shall make, before leaving the church, a declaration of mutual consent in his presence. It may be well to observe that the words of this declaration are sufficient to constitute a real marriage, if used by the parties with that intention. They will do well, therefore, to bear in mind that the act thus required to legalise their marriage in a civil point of view is a mere form to which they must submit as a legal necessity, but which adds neither force nor solemnity to the contract which they have already made in the presence of God and of His Church.

VI.

MORTUARY OBSEQUIES AND INTERMENT.

It is usual in all solemn commemorations of the dead to place a *catafalque*, flanked by six tall candles, in the choir, at which the Priest, after the celebration of solemn Mass, pronounces what is called the Absolution of the departed soul; or, on All Souls' Day, of the

Faithful Departed in general. Mass being ended, the Priest exchanges the chasuble for the cope, and standing with the Deacon at one end of the catafalque, remains there while the choir sings the piece called the 'Libera,' towards the end of which he places incense in the thurible, blessing it, and, after the choir has sung the Kyrie, intones the Paternoster, and then receiving the aspersory from the Deacon, makes the circuit of the catafalque, sprinkling it with holy water on either side, and bowing as he passes the Cross, which is borne by the Subdeacon at the opposite end. Having completed the aspersion, he receives the thurible, and again makes the circuit of the catafalque, incensing it, as before he had sprinkled it. Returning to his place, he sings the concluding words of the Paternoster, and afterwards the Versicles and Prayer of Absolution.

When the corpse is present, the same ceremonies are performed at the coffin as, in commemorative offices, at the catafalque; the Priest, however, always placing himself at the foot of the corpse.

The ceremonial of an interment is as follows: In Catholic countries the Priest and his attendant ministers go to the house of the deceased, and precede the corpse to the church, chanting the Miserere and other appropriate psalms. In our own Protestant land, where the free action of the Church is unhappily crippled, the Priest and Clergy meet the corpse at the entrance of the church, sprinkle the coffin with holy water, and then say or sing the 'De profundis,' or 'Miserere,' or both, with their proper Antiphons; then are sung or said the beautiful words, 'Come to [his] aid, ye Saints of God; meet [him], O ye Angels of the Lord, and receive [his] soul. *V.* May Christ, who called thee, receive thee, and may the Angels conduct thee into Abraham's bosom. *R.* Receive [his] soul, and offer it in the sight of the Most High. Eternal rest grant to [him], O Lord, and let perpetual light shine upon [him].' When the entire

Office is performed, whether at an interment or anniversary commemoration, the Matins and Lauds of the Dead are sung in choir, and, if at a funeral, in this place. High Mass then follows, with the Absolution before mentioned. At the funeral of a Bishop, the Absolution is given by the several attendant Bishops in succession. When the corpse is that of a Priest, the head of the coffin is placed towards the Altar; in case of another, it is the reverse. It is sometimes the practice to place on the coffin of a Priest the chalice, paten, and other insignia of his office, and the Priest is interred in the sacred vestments. When the Absolution is ended, the corpse is carried to the grave, the choir singing the following beautiful words: 'May the Angels conduct thee into Paradise; at thine approach may the Martyrs receive thee, and lead thee into the Holy City Jerusalem; may the Choir of Angels receive thee; and with Lazarus, who was once poor, mayest thou have eternal rest!'

When the grave is reached (if the cemetery be not consecrated), the Priest will bless it according to a prescribed form; but as the great increase in the number of our cemeteries now leaves no excuse to Catholics for omitting to comply with the rule and practice of the Church, which require that the Faithful shall be interred in consecrated ground, this exceptional provision is daily becoming less and less necessary.

When the corpse has been placed by the side of the grave, the Priest puts incense into the thurible and incenses the corpse and the grave. The chanters in the meanwhile intone the Antiphon, 'I am the Resurrection and the Life,' with the words following. Then is sung the 'Benedictus,' and the corpse is lowered into the grave, and earth cast upon it. After the Antiphon has been repeated, the Priest says the Kyrie eleïson and Paternoster, during which he sprinkles the corpse with holy water, and then continues the office to the end.

On returning from the grave, the 'De profundis' is said in a low voice by the Priest and attendants.

VII.

THE INTERMENT OF CHILDREN.

It is the beautiful custom of the Church to inter children under seven years of age with every mark of joy and thankfulness. Since it may be presumed that at that age they have not lost their baptismal innocence, the Church regards their death as a certain and immediate passage to glory, and does not allow any word or token of mourning to mar the brightness of the rite which she appoints for consigning them to the grave. The vestments of the Priest are white; flowers are strewn before the corpse, which is frequently borne by children also arrayed in white. The procession is introduced into the church, not, as in other cases, with penitential psalms, but with such as are expressive of the praise which children offer to God, or of the high privileges and exalted destiny of unsullied innocence. When the 112th and 23d Psalms have been said or chanted, the Priest says or sings the Kyrie eleïson and Paternoster, during which he sprinkles the corpse. Then is said or sung a prayer for the gift of innocence like to that of the child about to be interred. On the way to the grave is sung the most joyful of the Psalms of David, the 148th. On reaching the grave, the Priest says or sings the Kyrie and Paternoster, with the following versicle and response: *V.* 'Suffer little children to come unto Me.' *R.* 'For of such is the Kingdom of Heaven.' Then follows a prayer of like import with the preceding; after which the Priest sprinkles and incenses the corpse, which is then lowered into the grave. The Priest and procession afterwards return into the church, reciting the Canticle of the Three Children, 'Benedicite.' On reëntering the church, the Priest goes before the Altar and says the prayer appointed for the Feast of St. Michael and All Angels, as if to indicate that the soul of the little innocent, whose pure body has just been committed to the grave, has already passed into the company of those Angels who behold the Face of God, and fulfil holy ministries for the benefit of men.

VIII.

ORDINATION.

There are seven Orders in the Church,—besides the First Tonsure, which is not an Order, but only the act of initiation into the Ecclesiastical State, and therefore the preliminary condition of all the Orders,—which are as follow: 1. The Order of Ostiary or Porter; 2. the Order of Lector or Reader; 3. the Order of Exorcist; 4. the Order of Acolyth; 5. the Holy Order of Subdeacon; 6. the Holy Order of Deacon; 7. the Holy Order of Priest.—N.B. The Episcopate is not an Order distinct from the Priesthood, but is its plenitude, though requiring a special act of consecration, and involving powers peculiar to itself. We will begin with

The First Tonsure.

The First Tonsure can be conferred on any day, at any hour, and in any suitable place, upon those whom the Bishop judges to be duly qualified for admission to the Ecclesiastical State. The ceremony is as follows: Each candidate is habited in cassock, and carries a surplice on his left arm, and a candle in his hand. The Bishop, after the preliminary versicles and responses, calls upon those present to pray that the candidates may receive grace to renounce the world in spirit as well as in form, and to persevere in the state of life to which they have been called. The 15th Psalm is then chanted, with its proper antiphon. As soon as the

Psalm begins, the Bishop cuts off a portion of hair from the head of each candidate in four different places, while the candidate repeats with him from the fore-mentioned Psalm, 'The Lord is the portion of mine inheritance and of my chalice; Thou art He who shalt restore to me mine inheritance.' It is in these words that the youthful ecclesiastic takes God for his portion, while his renunciation of worldly things is symbolised by the act of cutting off the hair. When all have been tonsured, the Bishop recites the prayer; after which is chanted the 22d Psalm, with its antiphon. At its close the Bishop invests each of the candidates with the surplice, and, after a prayer, admonishes them to prize and act up to the privileges of their new state.

The Four Minor Orders.

The Four Minor Orders can be conferred, either in or out of Mass, on any Sunday or Double Festival; but, unlike the first Tonsure, in the morning only. It will be unnecessary to do more than describe the characteristic ceremonies of each of these Ordinations, without entering into a detail of those general features which they possess in common with one another and with the form of admission to the Tonsure. The essence of each of the four Minor Orders consists in the delivery of certain instruments or insignia of the particular Order conferred, and which the candidate is required to touch.

The Order of Ostiary or Porter is conferred by delivering to the candidate the keys of the church, which he is required to touch. He is afterwards conducted to the door of the church or sacristy, which he locks and re-opens, and afterwards sounds the bell of the church.

The Order of Lector or Reader is conferred by delivering to the candidate the Book of Lessons, which he is required to touch.

The Order of Exorcist is conferred by delivering to

the candidate the Book of Exorcisms, which may be either the Pontifical or Missal, and which he also is required to touch.

The Order of Acolyth is conferred by presenting to the candidate first of all a candlestick containing an unlighted candle, and afterwards an empty wine-cruet, both of which he is required to touch.

The appropriate duties of each of these ancient Orders are expressed by their different characteristic insignia. The duty of the Porter was to guard the entrance of the church, admitting the worthy and excluding the unworthy, as well as to summon the Faithful to the Divine Offices by sounding the bell. Hence at his ordination he receives the keys of the church and exercises his office. The duty of the Lector was, and still is, to read the Lessons in the Divine Office. Hence it is that he receives the Book of the Lessons at his ordination. The duty of the Exorcist was to exorcise the possessed, an office which, according to the present discipline of he Church, has ceased to belong to any of the inferior Orders; but it is in the reception of this Order that the Priest receives the power which he alone can exercise. The Order of Acolyth, like that of Lector, represents a really existing clerical office, that, namely, of assisting with the cruets at the Holy Sacrifice of the Mass; although, according to the actual practice of the Church, this office, like those of the Porter and Lector, is often discharged by persons who are not clerics.

The Holy Order of Subdeacon.

The Subdiaconate is the lowest of the three Sacred Orders, and involves the obligation of celibacy, and of the daily recitation of the Divine Office. The candidates are required to be vested in *Amice*, *Alb*, and *Girdle*, carrying on their left arms the maniple and *Tunic*, with which they are afterwards to be invested, and in the right hand a candle. They are summoned by name, and the title of their Ordination specified, whether it be the service of the diocese, private patrimony, or Religious poverty. The Bishop, at a certain part of the Mass, takes his seat before the middle of the Altar. The candidates are summoned before him, and addressed by him on the serious and irrevocable nature of the step they are about to take. The Litanies of the Saints are afterwards chanted, and all the candidates for the several Holy Orders who are present prostrate on the ground during their recitation. After the petition for the faithful departed, the Bishop rises, and pronounces three special supplications for the benediction, sanctification, and consecration of the candidates. The Litanies being ended, the Bishop instructs the candidates for the Subdiaconate in the duties of their office, which are chiefly to assist the Deacon in the Holy Sacrifice, and to wash the sacred linen used in the Mass. The address being ended, the Bishop delivers to each an empty chalice and paten to be touched, reminding them, in the form of words used in the delivery, of the greatness of the ministry thus committed to them. The cruets (containing wine and water) are then delivered to be touched by each candidate, and afterwards the basin and towel used in washing the fingers of the Priest at Mass. The Bishop then invites a prayer for the newly ordained. He afterwards draws over the head of each the amice previously borne on the neck, and invests them with the maniple and tunic; after which he delivers to each the Book of Epistles to touch. The Subdeacons then withdraw, and one of them sings the Epistle of the Mass, and the Bishop continues the Mass to the point at which he returns to his seat to administer

The Order of Deacon.

Those who are admitted to the Order of Deacon undoubtedly receive the Sacrament of Orders, and the rite has certain features of solemnity which do not belong to the preceding Ordinations. Among these are a solemn Preface, chanted by the Bishop with extended hands; at the end of which he imposes his right hand on the head of each candidate, saying the words, 'Receive the Holy Ghost for strength and power to resist the devil and his temptations, in the name of the Lord.' The Bishop then continues the Preface to the end, and afterwards invests the Deacons with the ensigns of their Order. They are already vested in amice, alb, girdle, and maniple, and carry on their left arms the stole and dalmatic. The Bishop invests them first with the stole, which is placed on the left shoulder, and fastened under the right arm. He then places on each the dalmatic, and afterwards delivers to each the Book of the Gospels to be touched. The Gospel of the Mass is sung by one of the newly-ordained Deacons.

The Subdeacon thus acquires by his Ordination the official right to touch the holy vessels and linen after the Blessed Sacrament has come into contact with it. This power, which he possesses in virtue of his Ordination, has been extended by custom to other Ecclesiastics, and can be given by the Ordinary to Sacristans, even though not Ecclesiastics. The Deacon acquires by his Ordination the right to touch vessels, even when they contain the Blessed Sacrament. The Deacon may also receive from the Bishop the faculty to preach.

The Ordination of Priests.

The Deacons who are to be ordained to the Priesthood wear all the vestments of their Order, except the dalmatic, in the place of which they carry the chasuble on their left arm. The Litanies are always chanted with the same ceremonies as have been described under the Ordination of Subdeacon when any of the Sacred Orders are conferred. After the Litanies, the Bishop silently imposes both hands on the head of each Deacon who is to be ordained to the Priesthood, and the same is afterwards done by every Priest present. The Bishop then, with extended hands, sings the appointed Preface. The Preface being ended, the Bishop places the stole on the neck of each, carrying the two ends over the breast in the form of a cross, and saying the words, 'Receive the yoke of the Lord; for His yoke is sweet, and His burden is light.' He then places on each the chasuble, but with the hinder part of it so folded as to cover the shoulders only. Then, after a prayer, the Bishop intones the hymn 'Veni Creator,' which is continued by the choir. After singing the first verse, the Bishop proceeds to anoint the hands of each Priest. kneeling before him, with the Oil of the Catechumens. The hands are afterwards bound together, with the exception of the fingers. The Bishop delivers to each the chalice, containing wine and water, and the paten with the bread, which are received and touched. The Mass then proceeds to the Offertory, during the singing of which, or before, the newly-ordained Priests wash the remains of the holy oil from their hands with water and bread-crumbs. Each one of them afterwards offers to the Bishop a lighted candle, as is done by all those who have been ordained, and then proceeds to say aloud with him the words of the Mass, beginning with those which are appointed for the Oblation of the Bread. The Bishop gives the 'pax' at the proper time to one of the newly-ordained in each Order, and he to the next, and so on, until it has been received by all, and the newly-ordained receive the Holy Communion. If Priests only be ordained, the Confession and Absolution prayers before Communion are not said, because they celebrate Mass conjointly with the Bishop, and are not therefore in the position of ordinary communicants. The newly-ordained receive a portion of unconsecrated wine after Communion as an ablution. When the usual ablutions have been received, the Bishop intones the following words, which are sung by the choir: 'I call you not now servants, but friends, because you have known all things which I have wrought in the midst of you. Alleluia,' &c. The newly-ordained Priests here recite the Creed as a profession of their faith. The Bishop then, imposing his hands on each, imparts to them the power of Absolution in the same words in which it was given by our Lord to the Apostles, at the same time lowering the hinder part of the chasuble, which had been previously folded up. Each of the Priests then places his joined hands within the hands of the Bishop, promises him reverence and obedience, and the Bishop gives him in return the kiss of peace. Finally the Bishop warns the newly-ordained Priests of the awful and perilous nature of the Sacrifice they are now empowered to offer, and admonishes them to take counsel of the more experienced of their brethren as to the manner of offering it.

It should be observed that, although Priests receive the power of Absolution at the time of their Ordination, they cannot exercise that power till they have received the necessary faculties or jurisdiction from the Bishop

IX.

CONSECRATION OF A BISHOP.

On the day appointed for the Consecration, which will be either a Sunday or high-class festival, two Altars are prepared, one for the consecrating Bishop, and the other for the Bishop Elect. That for the Bishop Elect will have two large candlesticks with lighted candles, and upon it will be placed the episcopal vestments (including a cope), which will be white, even though the colour of the day be different. The Altar for the Consecrator will be larger, and furnished with six (or at least four) large candlesticks, while all that is necessary for the ceremony will be placed on credence-tables. Two Bishops are required to unite with the Consecrator in the act of consecrating the Bishop Elect. The rite begins by the senior of the two assisting Bishops petitioning the Consecrator to proceed to the consecration; upon which the Consecrator demands the Papal Mandate, which is handed to him and read by him. The Elect then recites on his knees the episcopal oath, but this is sometimes taken in the Sacristy, or in a private chapel, before the public ceremony. The oath having been read by the Elect, and taken on the Holy Gospels, the Consecrator proceeds to interrogate him in a series of questions upon the duties of the momentous office to which he is called. This examination being ended, the Consecrator begins the Mass at the foot of the Altar (the Elect at first standing by his side), and proceeds with it as far as the Alleluia, or last verse of the Tract or Sequence exclusively. In the mean time, the Elect has been conducted by the assisting Bishops to his own chapel, where, being divested of the cope which he has previously worn, he assumes the episcopal vestments of the Mass, and proceeds to say it simultaneously with the Consecrator, and up to the same point with him. A prayer for the Bishop Elect is added to the Collect of the day. The two Masses having proceeded to the last verse of the tract or sequence exclusive, the Consecrator takes his seat before the middle of the Altar, and the Elect is brought into his presence by the two assisting Bishops. The Consecrator then instructs the Elect on the office of a Bishop. He afterwards invites those present to pray that the Elect may receive strength from God for the discharge of his office. All then kneel, except the Elect, who prostrates on the ground at the left of the Consecrator. The Litanies of the Saints are then chanted as far as the petition, 'Ut omnibus fidelibus defunctis,' &c. inclusive, after which the Consecrator rises (as in the rite of Ordination) and sings three special petitions for the Elect; praying the first time that he may be 'blessed,' the second that he may be also 'sanctified,' and the third that he may also be 'consecrated,' making on each occasion the sign of the Cross over him. The Litanies being ended, the Consecrator places the open Book of the Gospels on the neck and shoulders of the Elect, where it continues to be held. Afterwards the Consecrator and assisting Bishops impose their hands on the head of the Elect, saying the words of consecration, 'RECEIVE THE HOLY GHOST;' after which the Consecrator says a short prayer for the Divine blessing. The Consecrator then, extending his hands, sings the Preface; after which, kneeling at the foot of the Altar, he intones the first words of the hymn 'Veni Creator,' which the choir continues. The first verse of the hymn being ended, the Consecrator takes his seat before the middle of the Altar, and anoints with the Holy Chrism the head of the Elect, making afterwards with his right hand the sign of the Cross over it. He then recites a long and most beautiful prayer for the Divine grace and benediction, after which he intones the antiphon from the 132d Psalm, which the choir takes up and continues. He next anoints the joined hands of the Elect in the same form as at the Ordination of a Priest, using, however, the Chrism instead of the Oil of the Catechumens, and afterwards binds them together with a linen cloth with which the Elect had been previously invested. The Consecrator next blesses the crosier (if not previously blessed), and delivers it with a form of words to the Elect, who receives it between the fingers. He then delivers to him in the same manner the Episcopal Ring, placing it on the fourth finger of the right hand. He next takes the Book of the Gospels from the shoulders of the Elect, and delivers it to him closed; the Elect touches the Book, but without opening his hands, which have remained bound since they were anointed. The

Consecrator then, as well as the assisting Bishops, give to the Elect the kiss of peace. The Elect is then conducted to his own chapel, where his head and hands are purified after the Unction, and the Consecrator proceeds with the Mass as far as the Offertory, as does also the Elect. The Offertory having been said, the Consecrator takes his seat before the middle of the High Altar, where the Elect, having been conducted into his presence by the assisting Bishops, makes an offering to him of two large wax candles lighted, two loaves and two small barrels of wine (the loaves and barrels being silvered and gilt), at the same time reverently kissing the Consecrator's hand. The Consecrator then proceeds to the Altar and continues the Mass, saying all the words aloud. The newly-consecrated Bishop goes to the same Altar, and there, standing at the Epistle side between the two assisting Bishops, says the words of the Mass simultaneously with the Consecrator, from another Missal. When the first of the three prayers before Communion has been said, the Consecrator gives the kiss of peace to the Consecrated, and he to the assisting Bishops. When the Consecrator has received the Body and Blood of our Lord, he communicates the Consecrated from the same Host and chalice.* The Consecrated afterwards goes to the Gospel side of the Altar, and continues the Mass with the Consecrator, who is now on the Epistle side. When the Mass is ended, the Consecrator takes his seat at the middle of the Altar, and places the mitre, previously blessed, on the head of the newly-consecrated Bishop. He afterwards places on his hands the episcopal gloves, previously blessed, accompanying both acts by the prescribed words of presentation. The Consecrator then rises, and enthrones the new Bishop in his own seat, or, should

* Both Catalano and Morinus interpret the Rubric of the Pontifical as determining that one Host only shall be consecrated for the Communion of the two Bishops.

the Bishop be consecrated in his cathedral church, in the throne which he is afterwards to occupy; giving at the same time the crosier into his left hand. The Consecrator then intones the 'Te Deum,' which is continued by the choir. When the hymn begins, the new Bishop is conducted by his assistant Bishops through the church, and blesses the people as he proceeds; he then returns to his seat, where he remains till the hymn is ended. A short verse is afterwards sung, and the Consecrator recites the prayer appointed in the Missal to be used for a Bishop. Finally, the newly-consecrated Bishop, genuflecting at the Epistle corner of the Altar, salutes his Consecrator in the words 'Ad multos annos,' which he repeats three times on his knees, each time in a higher tone of voice, and when he has sung them for the third time, the Consecrator and assisting Bishops exchange with him the kiss of peace. The office concludes with the Gospel of St. John, which is said both by the Consecrator and the newly-consecrated Bishop.

X.

CONCLUSION.

And now, kind reader, you have before you, in as complete a form as consists with the limits of my work and ability, a picture of Catholic Worship in those solemn Offices and public Devotions of the Church, which Catholics are most apt to frequent, and strangers to witness. Imperfect as this representation is, it will suffice to exemplify and illustrate the careful forethought and reverential precision with which the Church everywhere provides for the honour of her Lord, and of all which in any way relates to Him. That complex assemblage of rubrical provisions in which the eye of an uninstructed curiosity often sees nothing but a collection of useless and unmeaning forms, is to the Catholic heart the visible expression of certain great principles, which the Church loves to impress upon her children in every manifestation of her spirit. Among these principles may be specified: 1. The reverential love of God and of His Saints. 2. The ineffable dignity and sanctity of His Presence in the Most Holy Sacrament. 3. The honour due to His consecrated servants, and to all who minister at His Altar. 4. The holiness required of those who enter His House, and especially of such as come near His Tabernacle. 5. The exact perfection to be studied in all that relates to His service. 6. The charity and courtesy which should mark the intercourse of Christians. The Ceremonial of the Church is in truth the transcript of her Faith, the epitome of her laws, and the mirror of her mind. And if even one inquirer shall be led by this little work to regard and study it under this aspect of its character, the chief object of the writer will have been accomplished.

TO THE HOLY CATHOLIC CHURCH.

Mother of Saints! how beautiful thou art!
In speech how gracious, how august in mien!
Guide of the conscience, Mistress of the heart,
In all thy steps confess'd a Sov'reign Queen!

There are who deem thy comely pomp a show,
Thy ceremonies gauds for children meet;
Vainly they prate to me, for well I know
How lovely are thy courts, thy words how sweet.

Kings have their marshals, palaces their state,
E'en Christian homes their daily courtesies;
For Rev'rence doth on Love obsequious wait,
And Love that lacks respect decays and dies.

And shall Thy Home, O King of kings, alone
No tokens of Thy Majesty display?
Shall no glad courtiers muster near Thy throne,
No duteous escort guard Thee on Thy way?

Forbid it, Lord! nor let the world intrude
Her lawless maxims on Thy virgin code;
Nor sullen Heresy with whisp'rings crude
Break on the stillness of Thy star-lit road.

Each symbol of Thy Presence, Lord, is dear:
The holy vessel, and the costly vest;
The Altar, where Thy Spirit comes so near;
The Tabernacle, where Thou deign'st to rest.

But chiefly dear, because to Thee most nigh,
Thy Priests and Levites, princes of Thy choice,
And they who at Thy Board their service ply,
And they who lift in choir the gladsome voice.

By rev'rent gesture or by staid salute
Their faith they witness, or their fealty prove;
And yield, in measur'd forms and acts minute,
Their loyal homage of punctilious love.

And Thou, whose wakeful eye doth count the sand,
And track the sparrow as it falls to earth,
Shalt note, and recompense with bounteous hand,
Each least and lowest deed of Christian worth.*

* *Lyra Liturgica*, 'Holy Ceremonies.'

GLOSSARY OF ECCLESIASTICAL TERMS

USED IN THIS WORK.

ABLUTIONS. The wine, or wine and water, used in washing the chalice or the fingers of the Priest after contact with the Blessed Sacrament, and received by him after the Holy Communion.

ACOLYTH. A cleric who has received the highest of the Four Minor Orders, or a minister who, though not a cleric, discharges the offices of that Order in the High Mass. The minister at a Low Mass is usually called a Server.

AGNUS DEI. The triple invocation addressed to the Lamb of God in the Mass shortly before the Communion.

ALB. One of the sacred vestments, consisting of a long linen robe, worn in the Mass and some other solemn Offices by all in Holy Orders.

ALTAR OF REPOSE. The Altar at which the Most Holy Sacrament is reserved during part of Holy Thursday and of Good Friday; sometimes, though less correctly, termed the *Sepulchre.* Also an Altar on which the Most Holy Sacrament rests during a pause in a Procession.

AMICE. One of the sacred vestments, consisting of an oblong piece of linen, used by all in Holy Orders. Anciently worn as a hood on the head, and still so worn in some Religious Orders; but usually placed on the neck, and tied round the waist. The ancient use of the Amice is signified by the practice of touching the head with it before placing it on the neck. It is worn under the alb, or over the surplice.

ANTEPENDIUM. The movable framed frontal of the Altar, varying in colour according to the day or season.

ANTIPHON. A verse preceding and following a Psalm or Canticle, usually taken from it, and designed to suggest the spirit or intention in which it is used by the Church.

ARK. The special tabernacle in which the Most Holy Sacrament is reserved between Holy Thursday and Good Friday.

ASPERGES. The ceremony of sprinkling the people with holy water before the High Mass on Sundays throughout the year.

ASPERSORY. The brush or instrument used in sprinkling holy water.

BALDACCHINO. A canopy used for sacred purposes.

BAPTISTERY. The enclosed space near the entrance of a church in which the Baptismal Font is placed.

BIRETTA. A square cap worn by clerics.

BUGIA. The candle used in assisting the Bishop.

BURSE. The case containing the corporal.

CANON. That portion of the great Eucharistic Rite which comes between the *Sanctus* and Communion, and relates immediately to the Act of Sacrifice. *Canon* is a Greek word signifying a *rule*, and is here used of that rule, or set form of words, according to which the Church discharges this high commission of her Divine Lord. The term is also applied to the sacred book used in Episcopal Masses instead of the ordinary altar cards, and containing the *Canon* (whence its name) and all other parts of the Mass which do not vary with the day.

CAPITULUM. A short passage of Holy Scripture used in the Divine Office.

CAPPA MAGNA. A silk robe with a long train worn by Bishops.

CATAFALQUE. A mortuary structure representing a bier and coffin.

CATECHUMEN. A candidate for Baptism under instruction.

CELEBRANT. The Bishop or Priest in the act of celebrating the Holy Mass.

CHALICE. The sacred cup of precious metal used in the Holy Mass for the consecration of the wine.

CHANTERS (or CANTORS). The singers who lead the chant.

CHASUBLE. The outer vestment of the celebrant.

CIBORIUM. The vessel of precious metal in which the Most Holy Sacrament is reserved for the communion of the faithful.

CINCTURE. See *Girdle*.

COMMEMORATION. The memorial in the Holy Mass or the Divine Office of some Saint or Mystery other than that which forms the principal subject of the festival.

COMPLIN. The final or *complemental* Office of the day.

CONFITEOR. The public confession of sin made respectively by the Priest and people in the Mass or Office.

CONFRATERNITY. A holy association formed with the view of promoting some devotional object.

COPE. An ample vestment worn by the Bishop or Priest when officiating out of Mass, and occasionally also by others.

CORPORAL. A square linen cloth placed under the Most Holy Sacrament, or some vessel containing it; so called from its connection with the Sacred Body of our Lord.

COTTA. A surplice.

CREDENCE. A table placed in the Sanctuary for such things as are required at Holy Mass.

CREDO. The Nicene Creed said in the Mass on all Sundays and great Festivals, as well as on certain others of lesser dignity. It is so called from the first word of the Creed.

CROSIER. The staff or crook borne by Bishops in their own dioceses as a symbol of the pastoral office.

CRUETS. Small vessels for containing the wine and water used in the Holy Sacrifice.

DALMATIC. The outer vestment of the Deacon.

DEACON. A cleric who has received the second of the three Holy Orders, or a Priest discharging the office of that Order at the High Mass, or assisting a Bishop at a pontifical celebration. The term *Sacred* Ministers is applied exclusively to the Deacon and Subdeacon.

DOUBLE (Festival). A Festival of the higher rank. Double Festivals are either, 1. Doubles of the First Class; 2. Doubles of the Second Class; 3. Greater Doubles; 4. Doubles. The other classes of Festivals below the rank of Doubles are, 1. Semidoubles; 2. Simples. Days on which no Festival occurs are called *Ferias*.

ELEVATION. The lifting up of the Sacred Host and Chalice after consecration for the adoration of the faithful present at Mass.

EXORCISM. The prayer or act employed in adjuring the Evil Spirit to quit the human body or other created thing possessed by him.

FALDSTOOL (*i.e. Fold*stool). A stool which folds up, used by Bishops at episcopal celebrations.

FERIAL RITE. The rite, or form of celebration, proper

to a *Feria*. (See *Double*.) According to this rite, the Collects, Preface, Paternoster, and 'Ite missa est' in the Mass, are sung to a simpler tone than on Festivals.

FORTY HOURS (Devotion of the). A continuous exposition of the Blessed Sacrament between the High Mass of one day and the High Mass of the day but one following. The former of these High Masses is called the *Mass of Exposition*, and the latter the *Mass of Deposition*. On the intermediate day a solemn *Votive Mass* of Peace is sung at another altar than that at which the Blessed Sacrament is exposed. At Rome, and in some other places, this devotion is observed successively at the various churches throughout the year. In England it is practised between Ash Wednesday and Palm Sunday inclusive.

GIRDLE (or CINCTURE). A cord used with the sacred vestments for confining the alb.

GLORIA IN EXCELSIS. The Angelic hymn which follows the *Kyrie* in the Mass, except on penitential days, in *Masses of Requiem*, on *Ferias* occurring out of Paschal-tide, and in most of the *Votive Masses*.

GRADUAL. A portion of the Mass which follows the Epistle, so called because anciently sung on the *steps* of the altar.

HOLY WATER. Water blessed for religious uses. A portion of salt (also blessed) is mingled with it.

HOST (Lat. *Hostia*, a victim). The Most Precious Body of our Lord, present in the Holy Eucharist, or the Bread before it has been transubstantiated.

HUMERAL VEIL. A veil to cover the shoulders.

INTROIT. The opening words proper to the Mass of the day, usually consisting of a text from Holy Scripture, with the first verse of a psalm, and the Gloria Patri.

KYRIE ELEISON. The petition for the Divine Mercy nine times repeated after the *Introit* in all Masses. The Greek form of the words may be regarded as a symbol of the unity of east and west in the Catholic Church. A similar token of this unity occurs in the Responses to the Reproaches on Good Friday.

LAVABO. The portion of Psalm xxv. recited by the celebrant at the washing of the fingers in the Mass. The word is also used of the act to which these words relate, and of the small cloth used by the Priest in wiping the fingers.

LAUDS. The Divine Office of Praise following the *Matins.*

LUNETTE. A small crescent-shaped or circular frame, in which the Blessed Sacrament is placed for solemn Exposition, and which is fitted into the *Monstrance.*

MASTER OF CEREMONIES. The cleric, or other minister, charged with the general direction of the ceremonies in solemn celebrations, as well as with certain special duties peculiar to his office.

MANIPLE. A sacred vestment worn on the left arm during the celebration of Mass by all in Holy Orders.

MONSTRANCE. A stand of precious metal used for the solemn Exposition of the Holy Sacrament.

NOCTURN. One of the three divisions of the Office of Matins, so called because anciently, and still in many Religious Communities, sung during the night.

OSTENSORIUM. See *Monstrance.*

PALL. A square stiffened piece of linen, placed on the chalice at Mass.

PATEN. The sacred plate of precious metal on which the Host is placed at Mass.

PAX. The kiss of peace, given and received at the High Mass, and some other solemn Offices. Also the instrument sometimes used by Bishops for the same purpose.

PISCINA. A drain near the Altar for carrying off the remains of sacred liquids.

PREDELLA. The highest step of the Sanctuary, on which the Altar stands.

PREFACE. The solemn words of introduction to the *Canon* of the Mass, varying with the season.

RELIC. A portion of the body of a Saint, or of some substance which has come into contact with it, exposed or resented, after proper authentication, for the devout eneration of the faithful.

REQUIEM (Mass of). A Mass celebrated, with the appointed rite, for the Repose of the Departed, so called from the first word of the Introit. When the Office of the Dead as well as the Mass is sung, the ceremony is usually called a *Dirge.*

SANCTUARY. The enclosed space surrounding the Altar.

SANCTUS. The triple invocation of the Most Holy, Three Persons in One God, at the conclusion of the Preface in the Mass.

SEDILIA. The seats in the Sanctuary for the officiating Priest and his Ministers.

SEMIDOUBLE (Festival). See *Double*.

SEQUENCE. A hymn introduced into the Mass on certain days, and, as the name imports, *following* the Gradual. The Sequences are five: 1. The 'Victimæ Paschali,' for Easter week. 2. The 'Veni Sancte Spiritus,' for Pentecost. 3. The 'Lauda Sion,' for Corpus Christi. 4. The 'Stabat Mater,' for the two Feasts of the Seven Dolours. 5. The 'Dies iræ,' in Masses of Requiem.

STATIONS OF THE CROSS. A series of pictures, or other representations, of our Lord's Passion, or the Devotions practised before them.

STOLE. A narrow scarf worn by Bishops, Priests, and Deacons: by Priests, round the neck, and, when with the alb, crossed over the breast and confined by the Girdle; by Deacons, across the left shoulder and joined under the right arm; by Bishops, uncrossed, even at Mass.

SUBDEACON. A cleric who has received the lowest of the three Holy Orders, or one discharging at the High Mass the office of that Order.

TABERNACLE. The receptacle for the Most Holy Sacrament permanently standing on the Altar.

THURIBLE. A portable censer.

THURIFER. The minister of the thurible.

THRONE. The elevated stand on which the Monstrance containing the Blessed Sacrament is placed during a solemn Exposition.

TRACT. Certain verses, taken generally from the Psalms, substituted for the Alleluias after the Gradual in penitential seasons, anciently sung in a protracted and plaintive tone, whence the name.

TUNIC. The outer vestment of the Subdeacon, similar to the dalmatic.

VEIL. The outer covering of silk, or cloth-of-gold, placed over the chalice and paten, when not immediately in use at the Mass.

VERSICLE. A short verse, said or sung by the officiating Priest, and answered by the people in a *Response*.

VESPERS. The Evening Office of the Church.

VOTIVE MASS. A Mass of special devotion other than the Mass of the day.

www.ingramcontent.com/pod-product-compliance
Lightning Source LLC
Chambersburg PA
CBHW032243080426
42735CB00008B/976

* 9 7 8 3 3 3 7 2 8 6 4 0 8 *